Permission to Write a Brand Building Book

For Podcasters:
9 Myths Holding You Back from More Exposure & Making a Greater Impact

Laura Petersen

Copyritght © 2018 Laura Petersen
All Rights Reserved.
Creator & Host: CopyThatPops.com
Email: Laura@CopyThatPops.com

ISBN: 9781980765486
Imprint: Independently published

Author:
Laura Petersen, M.A.E.D.

Title:
Permission to Write a Brand Building Book

Subtitle:
For Podcasters: 9 Myths Holding You Back from More Exposure and Making a Greater Impact

Subjects:
Writing a Book, Podcasting, Storytelling, Self-Psychology, Media Exposure, Adult Education, Self-Publishing, Amazon Book Publishing, Amazon Bestsellers, Becoming an Expert, Success Case Studies.

Rights:
All rights reserved. This book or any portion thereof may not be reproduced or used in any manner whatsoever without the express written permission of the author except for the use of brief quotations in a book review.

Printed in the United States of America.

First Edition.

Disclaimer:
Although the author and publisher have made every effort to

ensure that the information in this book was correct at press time, the author and publisher do not assume and hereby disclaim any liability to any party for any loss, damage, or disruption caused by errors or omissions, whether such errors or omissions result from negligence, accident, or any other cause.

Cover Illustration by Jesh_Designs
Cover Illustration Copyright © 2018 Laura Petersen

For podcast nerds like me
who have more you want to do in the world.

Table of Contents

Introduction ... 1
Reader Bonuses ... 5

PART 1: DO I HAVE PERMISSION TO WRITE A BOOK? ... 6

Start Here: Take These Two Quizzes First! ... 8
    1. QUIZ ... 9
    2. The Un-QUIZ ... 11

PART 2: YOUR OBJECTIONS TO PART 1 ARE FALSE, SO LET'S BREAK 'EM :-) ... 14

How Needing Permission to Write a Book is a Part of a Vast Right-Wing and/or Left-Wing Conspiracy ... 16

Chapter 1
MYTH 1: "I already have a podcast, so I don't need a book." ... 22
    New Vs. Historic ... 23
    On-Going Vs. One-Time ... 25
    #1, #2, #5, and #10 = Amazon ... 27
    #Repurposing Is Your Best Friend ... 31

Chapter 2
MYTH 2: "But I need a publishing deal!" ... 34
    What Authors Actually Say About Publishing Deals ... 35
    Self-Publishing Is Cheaper Than You Thought ... 38
    Which Self-Publishing Platform Should I Pick? ... 41

Chapter 3
MYTH 3: "But 'real authors' don't self-publish!" ... 58
    Self-Publishing Facts ... 59

Chapter 4
MYTH 4: "Writing a book is so hard and kinda scary." ___ 61
   If One Or More Of These Aren't Scary, Then...You're Out Of
   Excuses ___ 62
   Sucking At Grammar Isn't A Valid Point Anymore ___ 64

Chapter 5
MYTH 5: "I'm not expert enough to be an author." ___ 66
   Chicken Or The Egg? ___ 67

Chapter 6
MYTH 6: "Everyone's published a book. I missed the boat." ___ 69
   Booky Stats ___ 70
   NOW Is the Golden Age of Self-Publishing ___ 74

Chapter 7
MYTH 7: "No one will buy my book, so it's not worth the effort." ___ 77
   3 Benefits of "Connection" ___ 78
   Okay, But What If It Helps ONLY ONE Person? ___ 81
   Okay, But What If Truly NO ONE Buys My Book? ___ 83

Chapter 8
MYTH 8: "I could NEVER hit bestseller." ___ 88
   What Is A Bestseller Anyhow? ___ 89
   33, Are You Kidding Me? ___ 97

Chapter 9
MYTH 9: "Amazon bestseller is meaningless, so why bother?" ___ 100
   Don't Hate The Playah ___ 101

PART 3: QUIETING THE 'SENIOR PRINCESSES' [I.E. HATERS INSIDE & OUTSIDE YOUR HEAD] ___ 104

Chapter 10 How I Overcome Self-Doubt & Haters ___ 106
   The Mean Girls ___ 107
   Senior Princess Oppression ___ 109
   Enter: The Senior Queens ___ 111

Lessons Learned ... 112

Chapter 11 My New Manifesto ... 115
"Print Your Own Shirt"! ... 116

PART 4: MY STORY: BOOK #1 AND BEYOND ... 120

Chapter 12 Sick Of Feeling Like a Nobody = Massive Action ... 122
Fall of 2016 Was A New Chapter ... 123

Chapter 13 Amazing Rewards! ... 126
Brand & Business Building Results of Bestselling Book ... 127

PART 5: YOU ARE NOT ALONE - 7 CASE STUDIES OF PEOPLE LIKE YOU ... 132
Case Study 1: Sabah Ali (College Student & Podcaster) ... 134
Case Study 2: Tom Camp (Musician, Podcaster, Digital Nomad) ... 141
Case Study 3: Mitch Durfee (Growing Public Speaker) ... 145
Case Study 4: David France (Superconnector & Philanthropist) ... 149
Case Study 5: Kolton Krottinger (Disabled Veteran) ... 154
Case Study 6: Jaya M.K. (Podcaster & Obscure Field Expert) ... 159
Case Study 7: Akbar Sheikh (Very Busy Entrepreneur) ... 163
See More On The Wall Of Fame! ... 168

PART 6: YOUR TURN, YOU AUTHOR, YOU! ... 170
Your Permission Slip ... 172
Next Steps ... 174

You are awesome.

Introduction

FUN FACT [added post launch]
This book hit #1 in four categories in the United States and one category in the United Kingdom the day that it launched. Many thanks to all the supporters and true fans of podcasting, writing, and building a brand for impact.

This "bestselling launch" can be yours too. And we talk more about it in Myth 8 and Myth 9.

WHY DID I WRITE THIS BOOK?

It is my STRONG belief that:

Too many podcasters (*as well as entrepreneurs, solopreneurs, bloggers, video makers, content creators, artists, business men and women, and generally interesting, funny, entertaining, and/or knowledgable people*) hold themselves back from sharing what they know with the world in book form.

If you resonate with the above and think, "Dang, I am holding myself back!"

Then, this book will shift your mind and you will come to feel free as a bird to step into the title of published author.

Why care though?

A book is the most powerful tool I know of to help you share your message further, gain instant credibility, get more exposure, build your brand, and make a bigger impact.

10 THINGS YOU WILL GET FROM READING THIS BOOK

1. You will feel joy in getting unbridled permission to write a book. [From me, and more importantly, from yourself.]

2. You will feel clarity and confidence in knowing that you *should* to write a book. And you are 'expert enough' already, just as you are.

3. You will see 'a book' in a whole new and less overwhelming way.

4. You will be convinced that writing a book is a great (and arguably, necessary) tool to share your message, grow your authority, raise the status of your personal brand, promote your podcast, and get more leads, traffic, and sales for your business.

5. You will discover how to make money from your book, delightfully, even if you don't sell any books.

6. You will realize how and why a traditional publishing deal is no longer better than self-publishing. It's not even at all needed or desirable.

7. You will stop worrying about grammar, spelling, punctuation, margins, formatting, and all the minutia around books that is weighing you down, stressing you out, and slowing your forward progress.

8. You will learn all about what a 'bestseller' is and how it is far easier to achieve on Amazon than you would have thought.

9. You will be armed with reasons why, despite #8 being true,

You are awesome.

it's still worthwhile to hit #1 in your categories on Amazon and be proud of doing so.

10. You can access some sweet [free] bonuses (see the next section for how).

WHAT'S INSIDE THIS BOOK?

• You will take 2 QUIZZES
• We will break through 9 MYTHS
• You'll be inspired by 7 CASE STUDIES.

Let's go!

MY PROMISE TO YOU

All I know is that...
• Life is too short to hold back
• You have too much to share with others to keep it all inside (or off platforms - like a book - outside your comfort zone)
• A book is an amazing tool (like fertilizer to grow everything around your podcast, brand, and business)
• You'll regret it later if you don't

If you have ever:
• Thought about writing a book...
• Dreamed about writing a book...
• Considered writing a book...
• Heard that writing a book was fun, smart, and/or cool (and want to be fun, smart, and/or cool)...
• Realized how a book can help you grow your personal brand, podcast, and business...

Then, you will get unabashed gumption to stop seeking permission (you have it!) and freaking write your book. :)

So, now is the time to read on and take action.

I promise that by the end of this book you will feel confidence, clarity, and conviction to become a proudly self-published (and dare I say, 'bestselling'?) author ready to leverage your book for more exposure and bigger impact.

I can't wait to see your book live on Amazon, you soon-to-be author, you!

~ Laura Petersen
@LaptopLaura

San Diego, CA
March 23, 2018

Reader Bonuses

WHAT BONUSES YOU GET:

• Access to all link outs of this book in one place
• A real photo of the "Senior Princesses" you'll meet in Part 3
• A real photo of me from high school
• Free 1-Hour Training Video on *How to Painlessly Write and Publish A Best Selling Book on Amazon... With No Experience...In Under 8 Weeks...With $0 in Ads*
• Free Facebook Group of like-minded new and aspiring authors who support each other before, during, and after book launch
• Free, helpful podcast episodes about books
• Epic blog posts to help you with all stages of your book journey
• 7 A's of Self-Publishing Checklist
• 5 Things You Must Do to Hit #1 Bestseller on Amazon
• And more!

URL TO ACCESS THE FREE BONUSES:
CopyThatPops.com/BookBonuses

Part One

Do I Have Permission to Write a Book?

You are awesome.

Start Here: Take These Two Quizzes First!

You are awesome.

1. QUIZ

Convincing you that you have permission to write a book the #1 goal of this book, so let's get right into it.

INSTRUCTIONS:

Take this quick 2-question quiz to see if you qualify to be an author.

1. Can you write and/or speak a language that others understand?

2. Do you have something of value to teach and/or entertain 1 or more people? (Stories, lessons learned, business-y how-to stuff, jokes, case studies, experiences, etc.)

SCORE YOUR QUIZ:

If you answered "yes" to both questions above, you hereby have permission to write a book!

ANALYSIS

Is it really that simple?

Yes!

But, you likely don't believe me yet.

There are loads of screaming haters, already established and old-fashioned authors clinging to the rules of yesteryear, feelings of self-doubt, and 'Senior Princesses' (see Part 3 for their story) who would tell you otherwise.

So, please take The Un-QUIZ next.

You are awesome.

2. The Un-QUIZ

Convincing you that you have permission to write a book is my #1 goal, so let's have you take this Quiz #2.

INSTRUCTIONS:

Take this quick 11-question quiz to see if you qualify to be an author.

1. Do you have a college degree in your subject matter for proposed book? [Bachelor's or higher]

2. Do you have a college degree in English (or your intended language for a book), Writing, and/or Literature? [Bachelor's or higher]

3. Do you have a college degree in any subject or field? [Bachelor's or higher]

4. Have you won awards for your subject matter work, research, writings, etc.?

5. Have you spoken on big stages and on TV about your subject matter?

6. Have you received approval and encouragement to write about your subject from other industry experts, gurus, and/or influencers?

7. Have you received approval and encouragement to write about your subject (or anything, for that matter) from opinionated family and childhood friends?

8. Would you say that you are 'a nerd for grammar'?

9. Do you have a mega-influencer lined up to write a Foreword for you and endorse your book?

10. Do you have a massive email list, healthy social media following, and/or commitment from Oprah for a feature on her 'favorite things' list?

11. Are you aware of (and willing to staunchly commit to) using font types, book page count lengths, page word counts, margin sizes, gutter sizes, and other arbitrarily old-fashioned, pre-determined 'standards' of booky things?

SCORE YOUR QUIZ:

If you answered "no" to any and/or all of the questions above, you *still* hereby have permission to write a book!

ANALYSIS

But, Laura, are you surrrrrrre?

Yes!

But maybe you still don't believe me yet...

You are awesome.

Those haters, already established and old-fashioned authors clinging to the rules of yesteryear, encroaching feelings of Imposter Syndrome, and 'Senior Princesses' (see Part 3 for their story, impact in my life, and lessons we can all learn) talk loudly and convincingly. We need more evidence to combat them.

So, please continue on to Part 2.

PART TWO

YOUR OBJECTIONS TO PART 1 ARE FALSE, SO LET'S BREAK 'EM :-)

You are awesome.

How Needing Permission to Write a Book is a Part of a Vast Right-Wing and/or Left-Wing Conspiracy

You are awesome.

Spoiler Alert: It's All A Conspiracy

DO YOU NEED PERMISSION FOR...?

If I were to ask you…

…"Do you feel like you need permission to *start a blog*?"
…"Do you feel like you need permission to *launch an Instagram page*?"
…"Do you feel like you need permission to *post on your Facebook wall*?"
…"Do you feel like you need permission to *create a website*?"
…"Do you feel like you need permission to *record interviews for your podcast*?"
…"Do you feel like you need permission to *record how-to video tutorials for YouTube*?"
…"Do you feel like you need permission to *make checklists and step-by-step instruction PDFs*?"
…"Do you feel like you need permission to *teach a webinar presentation*?
…"Do you feel like you need permission to *share lessons learned on a Facebook Live*?
…"Do you feel like you need permission to *coach clients over the phone or in person*?

My guess is that for most or all of the above you would say, "No, I don't *need* permission!" I'm awesome at that!

AND YET...

Over 80% of the people I work with or talk to about writing a book express fear of writing a book:
- Because of feeling Imposter Syndrome
- Because they 'aren't expert enough yet to write a book'
- Because they don't have a degree
- Because of a lot of reasons

Even I, an admitted nerd for writing, back in 2016 before writing my first book *didn't even consider* being an author because I erroneously assumed it was something I *shouldn't* do until I had X more year's experience in my podcast and business. ["X" is some arbitrary number that no one knows. It's just in your own head or from the unfounded opinions of others.] Or until I had some publisher offering me a book deal.

After three people I respected, in the span of one week, told me I *should* write a book to stand out from my competition and grow my authority, I finally decided to take action.

[You can read more of my own story of the book writing journey in Part 4.]

BUT THEN I REALIZED...

Once I started working on my first book, I realized that a book is just a long-form way of communicating information, stories, ideas, and maybe a few jokes (I try not to take life, podcasting, business, or myself *too* seriously).

So why all the fear around doing a book?

You are awesome.

As I mapped out my first outline, I started looking at the book as actually 15 blog posts (I had 15 long chapters — too many, if you ask me now) with a central theme that tied them together.

You could also look at a book as 10-15 repurposed podcast episodes.

Add some 'introductory' book-like stuff at the front and a 'conclusion' with some call-to-action stuff (the book should be a tool to grow your podcast, brand, and business — in my strong opinion) and there you have a book.

'What's all the fear about then?' I realized.

WHERE THE FEAR COMES FROM

Ahh!...School and society have trained us to *wait* to be selected as worthy to write a book!

Ahh!...Already traditionally published authors don't want more competition from people choosing themselves and self-publishing!

Ahh!...Traditional publishers don't want us to think we can do it without them!

Ahh!...Haters, trolls, and strongly opinionated (though potentially well-intentioned) friends and family are too scared or conditioned by outmoded schooling and societal beliefs to write a book themselves, so they discourage you too as well!

Ahh!...There's a conspiracy! :)

A NEW WAY TO LOOK AT A BOOK

If you have 10 podcast episodes on effective _____ for _____ (fill in your subject topic)…

…Who's to say you can't transcribe those, fill in any gaps, add some intro and outro chaptery pieces to it, and publish it as a book?

If you have 8 blog articles on the best ways to _____ (fill in your subject topic)…

…Who's to say you can't make those 8 chapters, write some intro and outro chaptery pieces to it, and publish it as a book?

If you recorded 6 amazing interviews with gurus in your field…

…Who's to say you can't ask the interviewees if they mind the interview being repurposed, transcribe those conversations, add intro and outro messages for each interview (and the interviews as a collection), and publish it as a book?

Hint: This is a smart way to get other people wanting to share and promote you book because they appear in it.

If you feel like conventional writing standards are too stiff…

…Who's to say you can't include made-up words like "booky" or "chaptery" in your book? #DamnTheMan

If you feel more confident speaking than writing…
If you don't have time to write…
If you don't like writing…

You are awesome.

…Who's to say you can't create a great outline for your book and then 'talk out' each chapter, record it for free (I use Audacity from AudacityTeam.org), transcribe it (Trint.com is $15 per audio hour), pay someone to clean up any transcribing errors (you can rope in a family or friend for free or find someone on Fiverr.com or UpWork.com for a reasonable cost), and publish it as a book?

ULTIMATELY

It is my belief that life is too short to let others tell you what you cannot do.

If you see value in writing a book for yourself, for at least one other person, for your podcast, brand, and/or for your business (which I gently assert that you should), then you 100% need to write a book.

Ultimately, if you are reading this, you should just freaking publish a book. :-P

CHAPTER ONE

MYTH 1: "I already have a podcast, so I don't need a book."

You are awesome.

New Vs. Historic

PODCASTS ARE NEW

I am an avid podcaster, I used to run a podcast production company, I wrote a book called *Copywriting for Podcasters*, and I am a lover of listening to podcasts.

I go to Podcast Movement, I spoke on the Podcast Cruise, and I attend podcast meet-ups.

So, you can see that I loooove me some podcasts! :)

However, podcasting is a relatively new thing. Sure, radio has been around forever, but podcasts are seen as new and different.

Being 'new' can be cool and trendy.

But, in many ways doing something that's "new" is not given as much weight and value as doing something that's "historic" and held up as a pinnacle of success for a long time.

BOOKS ARE HISTORIC

That's what a book is.

Look at being a YouTube star (newer, like a podcast) versus a Hollywood star (historic, like a book) as another example of this phenomenon.

For now, at least.

"Historic" signs of authority may lose their power altogether, but while book authorship still glitters like gold in the sunlight, I truly believe all podcasters need to diversify and 'show up' as (bestselling) authors too.

If for nothing else, being a published author will help you as the host (and your show, in general) to grow in credibility, brand awareness, and traffic.

You are awesome.

On-Going Vs. One-Time

PODCASTS ARE ON-GOING (Usually)

Podcasts are amazing content to create as an entrepreneur, a niche expert, and a hobbyist who would like to grow an audience to perhaps monetize their show.

Usually we think of podcasts and episodic or on-going.

My own show Copy That Pops releases every Tuesday. The episodes are short quick tips (about 5-10 minutes long) or interviews with experts (usually around 45 minutes long).

So, my argument here is that a podcast is a great medium to share regularly and consistently with your audience in more bite-sized chunks.

Where as…

BOOKS ARE ONE-TIME (Usually)

A book, on the other hand, is usually a longer format for communication that is a "one and done."

In my mind, there is a purpose behind having this type of content (and product to sell) for your audience as a complement of your on-going content in your podcast.

Take advantage of both.

You are awesome.

#1, #2, #5, and #10 = Amazon

#1 MOST POPULAR RETAIL WEBSITE IN THE UNITED STATES (Ranked by visitors in millions)

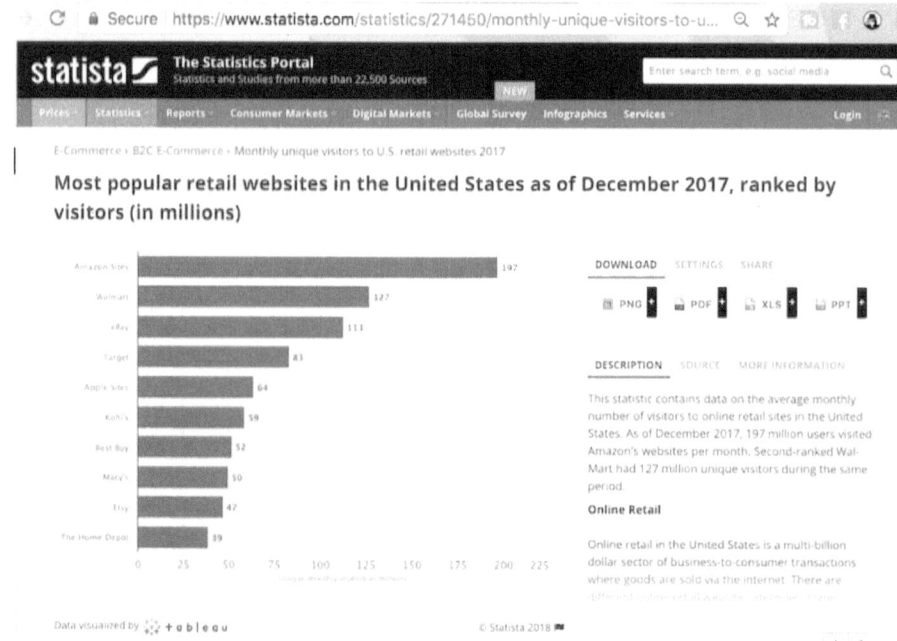

According to Statstica.com, Amazon is head and shoulders above all other retailers in the United States (as of the end of 2017).

(Source: statista.com/statistics/271450/monthly-unique-visitors-to-us-retail-websites)

#2 MOST INFLUENTIAL SITE OF ALL TIME

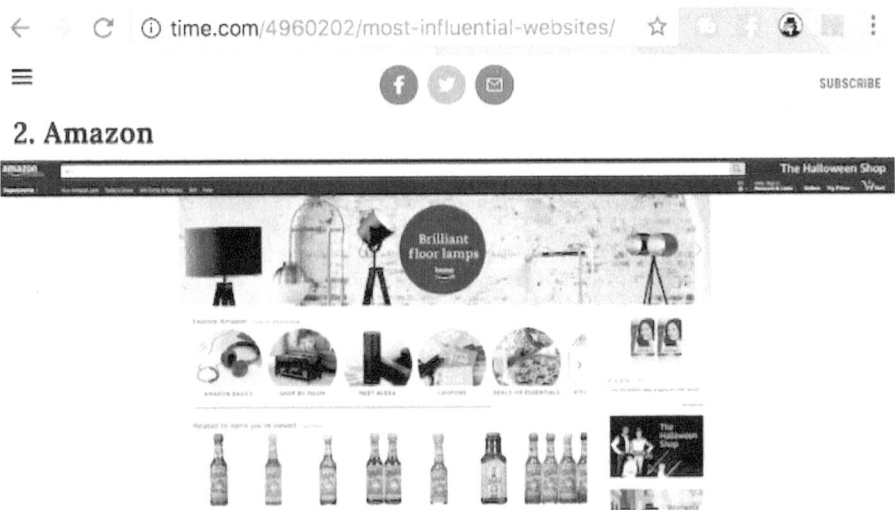

According to a *Time Magazine* article updated October 20, 2017, entitled "The 15 Most Influential Websites of All Time," Amazon ranked the highest, second only to Google.

(Source: time.com/4960202/most-influential-websites)

You are awesome.

#5 (in the US) AND #10 (in the World) MOST POPULAR SITES OF 2018

 The Top 10 Most Popular Sites of 2018

10 of 10 **Amazon.com**

Amazon is well on its way to being "Earth's most customer-centric company." The Amazon.com website offers a vast selection of retail products, including books, movies, electronics, toys and many other goods, either directly or as a middleman. Through its Prime service, it offers videos and music. It is the No. 1 shopping website in the U.S. with more than 600 million products available for sale. Globally, the site sells more than 3 billion products across 11 marketplaces.

Amazon is the No. 10 most popular global website in 2018. It ranks as the No. 5 most popular site among U.S. websites.

According to Life Wire, Amazon "is well on its way to being Earth's most customer-centric company."

If you want to attract more people to your podcast and business, you want to be in front of potential customers, right? Look no further to see where they head first when they need to buy something to solve a problem.

(Source: lifewire.com/most-popular-sites-3483140)

WHAT'S THE TAKEAWAY?

There's no question that Amazon is a behemoth. But by looking at some of these stats and article write ups, it should give you a better idea of just HOW big Amazon really is around the world and especially in the United States.

As a podcaster, if you are not searchable on Amazon, you are missing out on a lot of opportunities for brand awareness, new traffic to your show, sales of low-priced products (your books and other items), and new customers for anything else you are selling.

You are awesome.

#Repurposing Is Your Best Friend

YOUR PODCAST IS THE FOUNDATION OF YOUR BOOK

I like to say that if you have a podcast with 15 episodes that are 15 minutes in length, you have a book!

And those numbers aren't set in stone, by the way...

The point is that as a podcaster, you've already created a ton of valuable content for your audience. But what if a fresh audience is looking for answers (that you can provide) on Amazon but not iTunes?

Meet them where they are.

But, there's no point in reinventing the wheel from scratch to accomplish this.

You can transcribe relevant episodes (to fit in your book's theme) and turn those very shows into the book. Anywhere from bonus material, to a jumping off point to fill in more information, to the entire book.

Have some amazing interviews? Transcribe those and put them into the book word for word!

Make sure you have permission from your guests to reuse the content as you choose (something I recommend whether you write a book or not), and they will likely be ecstatic to get more exposure and status from being featured in your book that they will even share it with their audience when it's live.

TOOLS FOR TRANSCRIPTION

The tools that I have used include:
• Rev.com (about $60/hour)
• Trint.com (about $15/audio hour)
• Auphonic.com (I've just learned about this one a few days ago and haven't been able to fully test it. But there's the potential to get a good amount done free with syncing up Google Cloud's Speech API).
• Inside of Google Docs, when using the Google Chrome browser, you can activate their "Voice Typing" tool completely free. Google.com/docs/about

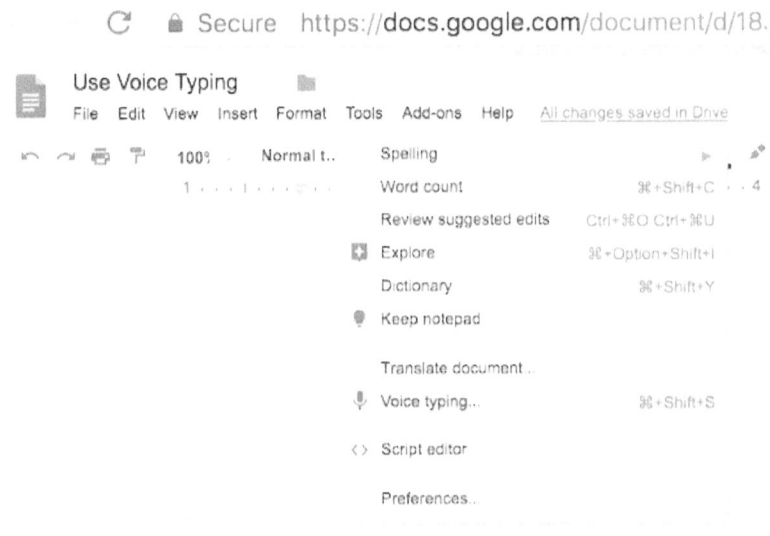

You are awesome.

STOP OVERTHINKING

'Everyone and their mom' has an opinion about what you 'should' do, what you 'can' do, and 'what a book is.'

Each person is entitled to an opinion, but it doesn't mean you have to listen to it.

Repurposing a value-packed podcast into a different form such as a book is not only legitimate, it's freaking smart.

Please ping me @LaptopLaura on social media or email me Laura@CopyThatPops.com if you repurpose all or part of your podcast into a book! I want to hear about it.

CHAPTER TWO
MYTH 2: "But I need a publishing deal!"

You are awesome.

What Authors Actually Say About Publishing Deals These Days

ARE YOU JOE ROGAN OR BUDS WITH BEYONCÉ?

If you are some big-time Hollywood star, renowned singer, or otherwise media darling, then a lucrative book deal could be great for you.

Mad props.

NOT YET A WORLDWIDE SUPERSTAR?

If you are anything like me or the clients I work with — podcasters, bloggers, entrepreneurs, niche authorities, content creators, business professionals — then you may have some kind of email list, social media presence, and/or recognition in your industry, but George Clooney and Tony Robbins don't have you on speed dial yet.

No worries.

Self-publishing is better anyhow!

Why?

Here are a few things you retain if you self-publish, but stand to lose if you sign a contract with a publisher.
• Total Control
• I.P. (Intellectual Property) Rights
• Speed
• Final Say in All Decisions (e.g., Book Cover, Word Choice, Launch Date, Pricing, etc.)

I have never done a tradition publishing deal myself — full disclosure — but in personally speaking with many who have, I can report that they have told me things like:

• "The publisher kept all the international publishing rights in the contract! So they get all profits for my book sold abroad."

• "The publisher took 18 MONTHS to get my book out! That was way too long."

• "I decided to do a traditional deal because I wanted to see my book in book stores and airports! And I know that is easier to achieve with publishing companies who have those relationships built. But, get this, over 80% of my sales came from Amazon anyhow. So was it worth it?"

• "Traditional publishers will only work to get their most well-known writers into bookstores [by paying for it]. If you aren't one of their most well-known authors, you're out of luck. They won't bother."

• "Good publishing deals are not available to you unless you already have a HUGE audience because they don't want to do any marketing for your book."

• "As a part of my contract I had to purchase $5,000 worth of physical copies of my own book."

You are awesome.

- "They forced me go with a book cover that I didn't want. I hate it."

- "I'm not actually sure what the publisher really did for me that I couldn't have done myself. And I'm not even able to login to my Amazon account and make changes. Is that 'normal'?"

- "I got a traditional publisher deal for my first book, but all future books will be self-published. I see no real advantage in traditional publishers anymore."

THE BOTTOM LINE IS...

If you want to write a non-fiction book to help grow your authority and make an impact, I recommend self-publishing 100% without any reservations.

Self-Publishing Is Cheaper Than You Thought

NO COST UP FRONT

In actuality, you can self-publish your book from start to finish for $0 up front.

How?

1. Do all these yourself or with the help of friends, family, or business services trade:
- Write
- Edit
- Format
- Cover Design

2. Set up an account with a self-publisher (my favorite is Amazon's Kindle Direct Publishing...see a very detailed explanation in the next section)! And you can make your Kindle e-book live to the world for $0.

3. Want to have a physical book available on Amazon too? Now, here's where you will have to shell out the big bucks! (Just kidding with 'big'). You can order a physical copy for yourself to do final checks 'at cost' + shipping (via KDP or Create Space, at the time of this writing). That is the only up front fee. We can say around $10 total for a book of about 150 pages.

You are awesome.

ROYALTY SPLIT

The way that Amazon makes their money is off a cut of any sales you make.

They give you 70% or 35% royalties for Kindle e-books, depending on a few factors:

- 35% royalties: Book must be priced between $0.99 and $200
- 70% royalties: Book must be priced between $2.99 and $9.99

For Create Space's printed books, it varies more based on number of pages in the book, if it's black and white or color on inside pages, the trim size of the book, your list price, etc.

From my test calculations, it's around 20-60% royalties. The way to maximize your cut of the money is to have fewer pages, print black and white interior, and raise the list price.

QUESTION: "ALTHOUGH IT CAN BE FREE TO START, WHY PAY FOR HELP?"

You may be asking in your mind, "Why pay for help, if I can publish my book for free?"

I believe we all have more time than money or more money than time. When you have more time than money, bootstrap and DIY every step! It's possible. I did it with my first book *Copywriting for Podcasters*.

Once you start feeling like time is more valuable than money, then you can get help for all the steps mentioned above, and

then some, like:
- Writing
- Editing
- Formatting
- Self-publishing platform set-up
- Great copy for your book's listing and author profile
- Marketing
- Timing and pricing strategy
- Strategic category selection in Amazon
- etc.

I've previously mentioned resources like AudacityTeam.org, Trint.com, Fiverr.com, and UpWork.com. These are great sites to get tools and/or help with audio recording, audio transcription, and formatting/editing help respectively.

You can also get help with cover design from Fiverr (which I used for the cover design of this very book), UpWork, as well as from 99Designs.com, Canva.com, and graphic designers in your network (feel free to ask me for recommendations too: info@CopyThatPops.com).

I also have free and paid tools to help you with writing, self-publishing, marketing, planning your launch, etc. [Learn more at CopyThatPops.com]

You are awesome.

Which Self-Publishing Platform Should I Pick?

TOP INDIVIDUAL MARKETPLACES FOR SELF-PUBLISHING

1. Nook Press (nookpress.com)
Nook is best known as the "Kindle of Barnes and Noble."

Even though they only distribute throughout the United States, they do offer an option to sell your print book on B&N.com, with the opportunity to sell it in stores.

As far as their transparency goes, I had to open a customer service case, posing as a confused author, to get a working link to info about royalties. When marketplaces keep info like *how much they're going to pay you* super-hidden, it sets off alarm bells (for me, at least).

Book options: Print book + ebook options
Manuscript format: Manuscript can be in .doc/.docx, .txt, .html, or .epub format
Cost to use: Free to DIY publish, email assistance if you have questions
Ebook royalties: If your ebook price is $2.99, you get $1.94 (65%)
Paperback royalties: Sell a $14.99 paperback on: B&N ($1.69)
Where they sell: Sell in the United States only
General transparency: Not great

2. Kobo Writing Life (kobo.com/us/en/p/writinglife)

To those that aren't familiar with Kobo, you might assume it's a distributor—but no, it's got its own marketplace!

Kobo is a digital book platform that reaches buyers across the globe.

They also have an "eBook Top New Releases" section. If you publish your book through Kobo ONLY and check your Kobo Writing Life Dashboard, you'll get updates about different promotions and you can submit your book for consideration to be included in the "Top New Releases" section.

Book options: Ebook options only
Manuscript format: Manuscript can be in .doc/.docx, .odt, .epub, .mobi format
Cost to use: Free to DIY publish
Ebook royalties: If your ebook price is $2.99, you get $2.09 (70%)
Paperback royalties: n/a
Where they sell: Global reach, but just on the Kobo e-store
General transparency: Good! Royalty info easy to find.

3. iBooks Author (support.apple.com/en-us/HT201183)

Personally, I still think of the iTunes store as a music marketplace or where I can search for podcasts [shameless plug to my Copy That Pops show found at copythatpops.com/itunes]—and *sometimes* my brain makes the leap to movies, like when I'm trying to watch *Legally Blonde* and discover that Netflix had the gall to take it down [it's a good movie, admit it].

But it's also one of the major platforms for authors selling

You are awesome.

ebooks—and the royalties are on par with most of the other distributors.

Their transparency is pretty nonexistent (not super surprising from Apple, king of trade secrets), but a few different people have written articles about it and included the royalty info.

(Sources: selfpublishingadvice.org/alli-watchdog-amazon-vs-apple and deirdre.net/writing/ebooks)

Book options: Ebook options
Manuscript format: Manuscript must be an .epub
Cost to use: Free to DIY publish
Ebook royalties: If your ebook price is $2.99, you get $2.09 (70%)
Paperback royalties: n/a
Where they sell: Global reach, but just on the iTunes store
General transparency: Not great.

4. Google Play (play.google.com/books/publish)

The only reason I'm including Google Play is because most of the aggregate distributors include Google Play as a platform, and I didn't want you discerning readers to think I'd left out a main marketplace.

Unfortunately, Google Play isn't currently (as of early 2018) accepting new sign-ups—so selling your book directly through Google isn't an option.

ROYALTY COMPARISON FOR INDIVIDUAL MARKETPLACES:

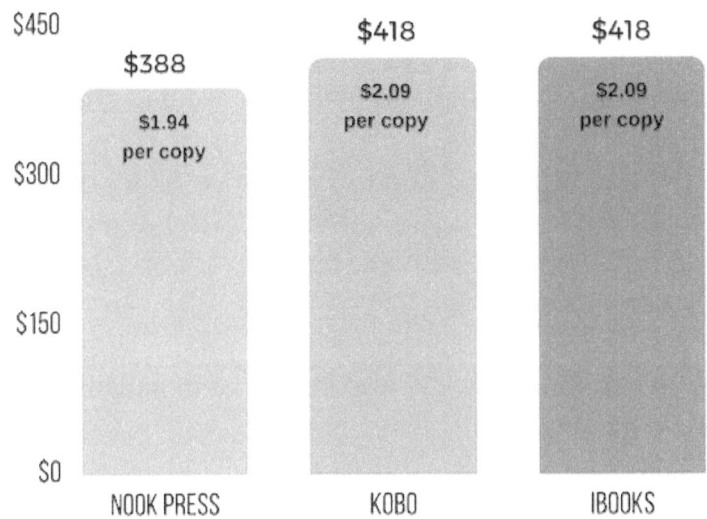

As you can see above, there's not a colossal difference.

Kobo and iBooks are tied for ebook royalties. But after selling 200 copies on each of these platforms, Nook Press would leave you with $30 less — money you could have *probably* used to buy some celebratory wine (or, for my tastes, celebratory rum and coke).

Now let's move on to…

TOP AGGREGATE BOOK DISTRIBUTORS FOR SELF-PUBLISHING

1. Lulu (lulu.com)
Lulu is an extremely transparent, user-friendly aggregate distribution service.

You are awesome.

They have "Up and Coming Author" sections and "Best Seller" sections, but the process of reaching those categories is a *little* unclear.

They also push your book across all the big marketplaces, including its own—and, of course, iBooks, nook, Kindle, and kobo.

The royalties get a little tricky, though. If you sell a $2.99 ebook on the Lulu marketplace alone, you get $1.80 (60%)—but you literally can't sell a $2.99 ebook on their other platforms, because you won't make any money.

You'd have to sell an $8.99 ebook, and you'd get diminishing returns as Lulu paid distributors' fees:
- Lulu ($7.20)
- iBooks ($5.66)
- nook ($4.05)
- Kindle ($3.46)
- kobo ($3.61)

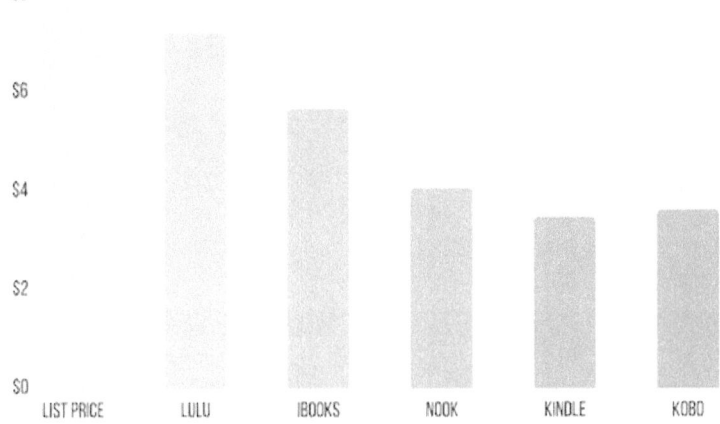

The paperback royalties are even steeper. If you sold a $14.99 paperback, these are the royalties you'd walk away with:
- Lulu ($7.76)
- Amazon/B&N/Ingram ($1.58)

You are awesome.

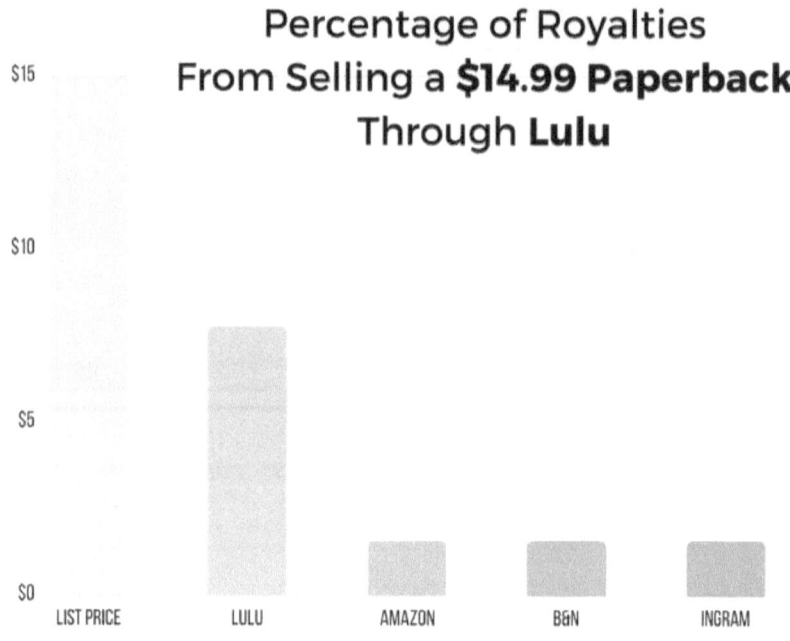

Book options: Print book + ebook options
Manuscript format: Manuscript should be in an .epub format
Cost to use: Free to DIY publish; paid packages available if you want help publishing
Ebook royalties: If your ebook price is $2.99, you get $1.80 ($0.99 hosting fee + 10% Lulu cut)
Paperback royalties: Sell a $14.99 paperback on: Lulu ($7.76), Amazon/B&N/Ingram ($1.58)
Where they sell: Global reach; Lulu, iBooks, nook, Kindle, kobo
General transparency: Great! Royalty info and merchandising info right up front.

2. Smashwords (smashwords.com)
Smashwords is another distributor that does things slightly differently. Aside from the big 3 (iBooks, nook, Kobo – NOT

Amazon, though), they have a handful of affiliates they sell to — and sales to these affiliates get you higher royalties.

They also sell to libraries and library aggregators.

If you sold a $2.99 ebook through Smashwords, here's what you'd get back on each of their platforms:
- Smashwords ($2.54)
- Affiliate platform ($2.11)
- Libraries ($2.09)
- iBooks/nook/Kobo ($1.79)
- Library aggregators ($1.35)

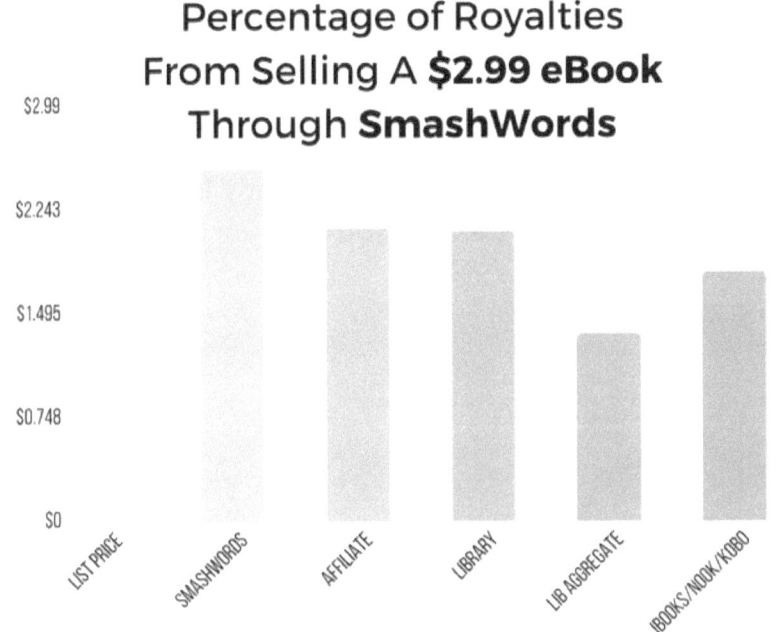

Book options: Ebook options only
Manuscript format: Manuscript can be a .doc/.docx — they convert it
Cost to use: Free to DIY publish (no packages available)

Ebook royalties: See chart above
Paperback royalties: n/a
Where they sell: Global reach; Smashwords, iBooks, B&N, Kobo, libraries, library aggregators
General transparency: Great! Royalty info and merchandising info right up front.

3. IngramSpark / Ingram Company (ingramspark.com)
IngramSpark is a HUGE distributor — an extremely massive company. They'll sell your book on Amazon, B&N, Apple, Kobo, and a ton of other digital and print retailers.

Unlike most of the other platforms, there's a setup fee to DIY publish–$25 for an ebook, or $49 for a print book or a print + ebook package.

The ebook royalties are fairly low; across the board, it's an even 40%. So if you sold a $2.99 ebook through any IngramSpark-affiliated marketplace, here's what you'd get:

- IngramSpark ($1.20)

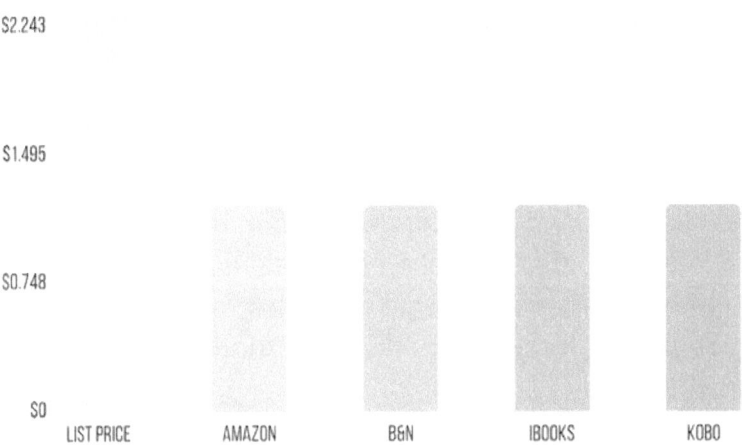

If you paid the setup fee, you'd have to sell 21 copies of your ebook before it paid for itself.

The paperback royalties are confusing and very hidden–they just say they pay between 45-75%, depending on the wholesale price, and they subtract manufacturing costs from that. But suffice it to say, you're probably walking away with a max of 40% of your list price.

That means a $14.99 paperback sale *might* net you $6.00.

Book options: Print + ebook options
Manuscript format: Manuscript must be an .epub file
Cost to use: Setup fee to DIY publish ($25 for ebook, $49 for print or print + ebook)
Ebook royalties: If your ebook price is $2.99, you get $1.20

(40%)
Paperback royalties: Sell a $14.99 paperback, you get back 45-75%, depending on wholesale price, minus manufacturing costs
Where they sell: Global reach; Amazon, B&N, Apple, Kobo, plus other digital and print retailers
General transparency: Not great–royalty info extremely difficult to find!

4. Draft2Digital (draft2digital.com)
Draft2Digital has kind of an interesting gimmick. They only sell ebooks, but they offer the option to create a paperback-ready file for you with auto-formatted front and back matter. That won't make you money through Draft2Digital, though–it's just a service they provide.

Otherwise, they're sort of medium-transparent.

Their royalties seem almost alarmingly high at first glance (85%), but then it becomes clear that they take a 15% cut out of your net royalties, NOT the list price. So whatever royalties you get from Barnes and Noble, for example, Draft2Digital skims 15% off of that.

That's all well and good–that's how a business works, after all–but it'd be nice to have some hard-and-fast numbers.

- Draft2Digital (at most $2.54)

Permission to Write a Brand Building Book For Podcasters

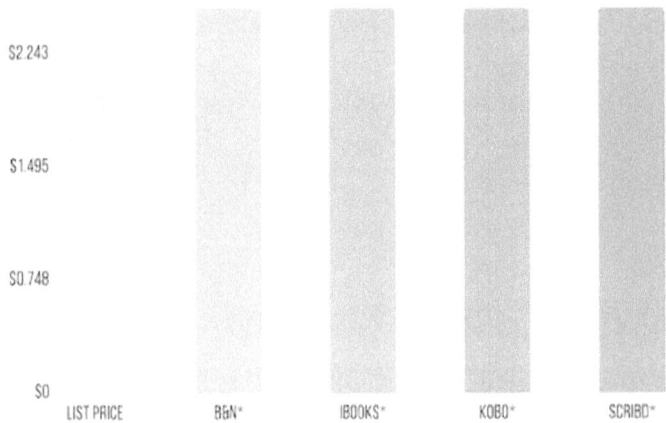

*Draft2Digital royalties may vary slightly--they take a consistent 15% cut of your net royalties, NOT the list price.

Book options: Ebook options only
Manuscript format: Manuscript can be a .doc/.docx, .rtf, or .epub
Cost to use: Free to DIY publish
Ebook royalties: If your ebook price is $2.99, you get, at most, $2.54 (85%)
Paperback royalties: n/a
Where they sell: Global reach; iBooks, B&N, kobo, Scribd, and more
General transparency: Okay, but not wonderful.

ROYALTY COMPARISON FOR AGGREGATE BOOK DISTRIBUTORS:

Since every distributor sells on different platforms at different percentages, the clearest way to compare ALL of them is through

You are awesome.

a common, well-known, global platform.

You get where I'm going with this?

Yep–I thought so.

Let's compare your royalty rates if you sold your book on Amazon through any of the listed distributors…and then, of course, through Amazon itself.

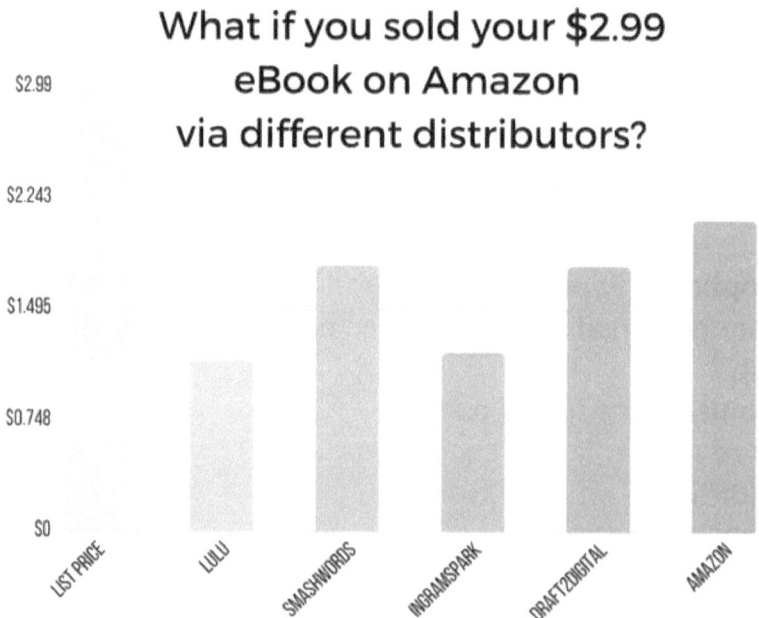

As it shows here, Lulu and IngramSpark are semi-tied for last place, and SmashWords and Draft2Digital are tied for 2nd place. Amazon comes out on top with 70% royalties.

Wait, so Amazon really offers the best deal, this early in the game? Well–in a lot of senses, yes.

It's time for…

THE BENEFITS OF SELF-PUBLISHING EXCLUSIVELY WITH AMAZON

Not only does Amazon legitimately offer a better deal than most distributors, but it has a global reach *and* it's a household name. (When's the last time you heard someone say, "I was shopping for new books on Kobo"?) :)

Aside from its initial street cred, though, there are three primary benefits to publishing exclusively with Amazon, and they'll *all* help you hit Amazon #1 Bestseller. No joke!

Here are two ways:
1. Wider exposure as described in each subsection below.
2. More favorable search/rankings results. Now, this isn't explicitly stated from Amazon, but I'm willing to bet that their algorithm favors books from authors who give them exclusivity. Food for thought!

Okay, the (clearly stated) benefits of listing your book exclusively with Amazon are:
1. KDP Select
2. MatchBook
3. Kindle Countdown Deals

1. What is Amazon's KDP Select?
First off, KDP stands for Kindle Direct Publishing and it's Amazon's ebook publishing arm of things (though at the time of this writing, they have printed book capabilities with some features still in beta).

You are awesome.

KDP Select is a sort of members-only program that you can join if you agree to (in a few quick clicks) sell your ebook (not your printed book) EXCLUSIVELY with Amazon for 90 days.

If you do, then your book is suddenly eligible for:

- 70% royalty earnings on sales to customers in Brazil, Japan, India, and Mexico
- Royalties from Kindle Owners' Lending Library and Kindle Unlimited (you get paid per pages read)
- Free book promotions (you can make your book free for a limited time, for example)

All of this? Awesome. But in particular, the free book promotions mean you can get more book "sales," which will open the Amazon #1 Bestseller door in the free lists in no time.

[Note that Amazon has different rankings for books that are free versus books that are $0.99 or higher].

And, since your book has SO MANY MORE benefits than just the royalty cut off sales alone, being able to give your book away for free on one of the largest websites in the world means a great opportunity for more exposure to your podcast, brand, and business!

Read more on KDP Select here on Amazon's site:
kdp.amazon.com/en_US/help/topic/G200798990

2. What is MatchBook?
Kindle MatchBook means that if a reader buys your physical book, they can get your ebook for $2.99 or less. Obviously, if you're launching immediately with an ebook, and not launching a physical book for a couple months, this won't immediately pay off, per se.

But when you *do* launch your physical book, you can offer a bundled deal that's immediately built in through the Amazon MatchBook program.

I say why not offer a print book reader a 'lil extra bonus to sweeten the deal?

Read more about MatchBook from Amazon's site: amazon.com/gp/help/customer/display.html?nodeId=201362970

3. What are Kindle Countdown Deals?
After you've been selling with Amazon exclusively for 30 days, you're eligible to participate in Kindle Countdown Deals. Kindle Countdown Deals are awesome discount deals that let you lower your price at specific intervals for a specific amount of time.

For example, let's say you normally sell your ebook for $6.99, and you want to run a 5-day promotion starting Monday at 8am and ending Saturday at 8am.
- Monday 8am: Price at $1.99 for 24 hours
- Tuesday 8am: Price at $2.99 for 24 hours
- Wednesday 8am: Price at $3.99 for 24 hours
- Thursday 8am: Price at $4.99 for 24 hours
- Friday 8am: Price at $5.99 for 24 hours
- Saturday 8am: Price returns to original list price $6.99

During each day the promotion runs, there will be a counter next to your book title listing the original price, the current price, the countdown, and the next price. This increases the urgency to buy your book at the low price, before the deal goes away!

There's also a dedicated website for these: amazon.com/kindlecountdowndeals. That's easier for customers and for you.

Plus, you can track the whole thing with your KDP report, which keeps a record of sales and royalties at each price discount alongside your book's pre-promotion performance.

Some Kindle Countdown Rules:
- You can't change the price for 30 days before or 14 days after your deal runs. (So you can't list it for free in the month leading up to your deal–but you CAN run a free promotion instead of your countdown deal.)
- During a Kindle Countdown, you can't sell your book for less than $1 USD.
- You can't split your countdown into more than 5 price increments.
- Your countdown must be scheduled at least 24 hours before it starts.
- The latest time your countdown can end is 14 days before your KDP Select period ends.

Read more about CountDown deals from Amazon's site: kdp.amazon.com/en_US/help/topic/G201293780

LONG STORY SHORT

While there are many options to self-publish, I recommend big 'ole Amazon. So, let the stress fall away, set up an account on KDP.Amazon.com and CreateSpace.com (Amazon will likely phase out CreateSpace as it adds more print version options inside KDP. In fact, I am testing out KDP's print capabilities with this very book!), and you are on your way.

[And remember, you can find all links in one clickable place back at CopyThatPops.com/BookBonuses]

CHAPTER THREE
MYTH 3: "But 'real authors' don't self-publish!"

You are awesome.

Self-Publishing Facts

SELF-PUBLISHING HAS ALREADY RISEN

According to research data from an Author Earnings' report in February of 2017:

In the United States:
• Over $3,177,000 is spent each year on ebooks.
• Nearly 80% of that is through Amazon.
• About 26% of ebooks were published with a "big five publisher" and 18% with a small/medium publisher (or about 44% with traditional publishing)
• About 14% were with Amazon Imprint and 34% as Indie Self-Published (or about 48% with non-traditional self-publishing)

Note:
The "big five publishers" are Penguin Random House, Harper Collins, Hachette, Simon & Schuster, and Macmillan.

(Source: authorearnings.com/report/february-2017)

There is also data from outside the US in this report. But the US stats were most dramatic and, I believe, an indicative trend of where things will continue to shift worldwide.

RECOGNIZABLE PODCASTER AND BUSINESS NAMES ARE ALREADY SELF-PUBLISHING

- Chris Ducker
- Danielle LaPorte
- Denise Duffield-Thomas
- Guy Kawasaki
- James Altucher
- James Malinchak
- John Lee Dumas
- Kim Kiyosaki
- Lewis Howes
- Pat Flynn
- Mark Schaefer
- Robert Kiyosaki
- Seth Godin
- Sharon Lechter

[Please email me more notable names for me to add to this list: info@CopyThatPops.com — thanks in advance!]

CHAPTER FOUR
MYTH 4: "Writing a book is so hard and kinda scary."

If One Or More Of These Aren't Scary, Then... You're Out Of Excuses

WHICH OF THESE THINGS ARE *NOT* HARD AND SCARY FOR YOU?

...Recording solo podcast episodes
...Recording podcast interviews
...Writing a blog article
...Writing a long post on Facebook
...Writing a white paper
...Creating great photos and engaging captions for Instagram
...Crafting a PowerPoint presentation
...Delivering a webinar
...Doing Facebook Lives
...Video recording interviews
...Video recording how-to videos
...Making checklists and step-by-step instruction PDFs
...Coaching clients over the phone or in person

If NOT A SINGLE ONE of these is 'easy and fun,' then you likely are in the wrong business, field, and/or life pursuit.

So, since 99.9% of you reading this will find at least one or more items on the above list palatable, then, you have a 'hack' for writing your book without the arduousness of writing it from start to finish.

THINK OF IT DIFFERENTLY NOW

Think instead how you can repurpose, record + transcribe, and hire help for ghostwriting, editing, formatting, or finding gaps you need to fill in.

It's time to stop putting a book on a pedestal as your life's crowning achievement. A book is simply a longer way to teach someone something to solve a problem in written form.

And it doesn't even have to be *that* long.

As you'll see in Part 5 with *You Are Not Alone - 7 Case Studies Like You* — my best-performing client to date Akbar Sheikh published his first book and it is around 61 pages printed (if we approximate about 220 words per page, that's like 13,420 words). He hit #1 bestseller in 6 countries.

If we stipulate that a 'long blog post' is about 3,500 words, then, this is less than 4 long blog posts.

Break this up over time, use repurposed podcast transcriptions, and it just isn't that daunting anymore!

Sucking At Grammar Isn't A Valid Point Anymore

SUCKING AT GRAMMAR *WAS* BAD FOR THE SAT'S

It's true that you may have deep battle wounds from school, standardized tests, and mean overachievers who teased you for mixing up "there," "their," and "they're" back in the day.

But…

WE WERE LIED TO IN SCHOOL

It wasn't a malicious lie!

It's just that the world has changed.

I was an übernerd in school and believed that contractions, misspellings, and ending a sentence with a preposition were the devil!

Where my nerds at!? :)~

[And SMILEY FACES IN A BOOK!? Blasphemy.]

But, a book is just a form of communicating information from one brain to the next. If it accomplishes that goal, does it REALLY matter if a few 'rules' of proper English (or, whatever language you will write in) are broken?

I'd never argue to put junk out into the world, no matter the medium.

But, we cannot let fear of a few errors (which can be fixed at literally any time, by the way — you CAN edit your book file with a few clicks) hold us back from sharing our ideas and knowledge with the world.

Perfectionism, especially around 'rules' that are arguably old-fashioned, is not the ideal.

BESIDES, THERE ARE WAYS TO MAKE ERRORS DISAPPEAR LIKE JIMMY HOFFA

There are editors for hire the world round.

Don't believe me?

Search "book editor" in <u>Fiverr.com</u> and <u>Upwork.com</u> and tell me what you see.

You likely have some nerdy friends from childhood who would love to spend a few Friday and Saturday nights proofreading your manuscript.

Stop letting "I suck at writing" slow you down.

CHAPTER FIVE
MYTH 5: "I'm not expert enough to be an author."

You are awesome.

Chicken Or The Egg?

FIRST OF ALL

• Are you expert enough to share what you learned on a podcast, video, blog, or Facebook Live?
• Are you expert enough to help clients with products and services related to your business?

Then, you are expert enough to pen a book.

But if you need more convincing…

WHICH CAME FIRST? THE CHICKEN OR THE EGG?

Let's look at the word "authority."

According to Dictionary.com:

> Word Origin and History for authority
> *n.*
> …from Latin *auctoritatem* (nominative *auctoritas*) "invention, advice, opinion, influence, command," from *auctor* "master, leader, author"

I would argue, therefore, that one *becomes* an authority by the act of *being* an author.

You had it backwards, yo.

If you have knowledge to share, then put it down in writing, publish it with the world, and earn your authority. Stop waiting for 'authority' to come to you, to be bestowed upon you patronizingly from some 'guru' in your field, or to be granted after waiting for an unending, out-of-your-control period of time.

You are already expert enough. Right now.

CHAPTER SIX

MYTH 6: "Everyone has already published a book. I missed the boat."

Booky Stats

KINDLE E-BOOK STATS

According to Amazon as of March 15, 2018 there are about 6 million Kindle E-books and 30,000,000 Paperback books available.

You are awesome.

Some of these books are overlapping (both a Kindle and Paperback of the same book), but we can go high and call it 36,000,000 books on Amazon.

BLOGS

According to (statista.com/statistics/256235/total-cumulative-number-of-tumblr-blogs) there are over 400,000,000 blogs *on just Tumblr* alone.

Over 4,004,655 blog *posts* have been written by 6pm PST (as I type this right now on Thursday March 15, 2018). worldometers.info/blogs

Even with these figures of say 4 million per day x 365 days (as a LOW estimate), that is 1,460,000,000 blog posts a year.

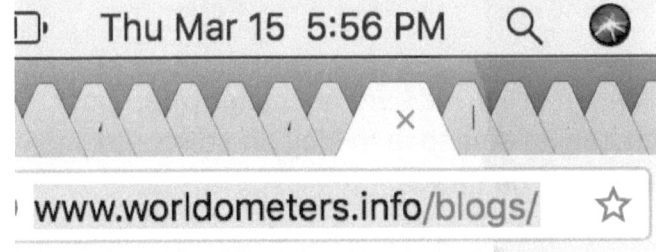

WHY COMPARE THESE TWO?

I bet if you told a friend or business colleague that you were starting to blog they'd encourage you and think it were smart.

Yet that same friend or business colleague may discourage you from writing a book.

And the overall competition for a book versus a blog (or even a blog post) is night and day!

I'd rather be:
- 1 of 6,000,000 Kindle E-books
- 1 of 36,000,000 Books

Than:
- 1 of 1,460,000,000 Blog Posts

REALITY

Standing out in millions or billions is hard no matter what. But I find the logic of encouraging someone to blog and discouraging them from writing a book to be flawed.

Plus, Amazon let's you browse by categories, subcategories, and keywords.

So, they make it *easier* to be found as compared to 1 blog in all of Google.

Take advantage of this while you can.

Right NOW Is the Golden Age of Self-Publishing

5 REASONS WHY RIGHT NOW IS THE PERFECT TIME TO PUBLISH YOUR BOOK

It is my contention that we are in the golden age of self-publishing as a podcaster and as an entrepreneur. As a content creator. As an artist. As a business owner. As a growing thought leader.

Right *meow*!

Here's why...

#1: "Self-publishing" is respected.

HUGE names are choosing to self-publish (like Pat Flynn, James Altucher, John Lee Dumas, and more! — See Chapter 3 for more folks).

This didn't use to be the case.

In the past, only people who 'couldn't' get a publishing deal self-published and it was looked down upon with mockery.

Now it's well-respected. [Let's all agree to ignore the outliers who are haters. Send me their messages and we can have a laugh at it together. You do you. I respect it.]

Today, thought leaders and biz gurus with giant audiences see the power of publishing themselves! They keep all their I.P. rights, get bigger royalty cuts, and can move light years FASTER than with traditional publishers.

#2: It's never been simpler.

There is a lot to research and decide when it comes to publishing a book, true (that's why I'm here to help save you time, stress, and confusion!).

But you can follow my proven steps and systems to write, self-publish, market, and leverage a book...that you CAN and WILL make a bestseller...even if you don't love writing, have never done it before, or don't have a huge audience.

It's straightforward when someone who's done it breaks it all down for you.

And, if you want to DIY it, you absolutely can.

#3: There is still MAGIC around books.

Saying, "I'm a published author" and "Yes, I wrote the bestselling book on that topic" turns heads, drops jaws, and widens eyes.

Even though 'anyone' *can* publish a book, it still has fairy dust all around it and has the magical power to open doors and expand opportunities.

It's the childhood dream of many people. Maybe of yours?

Being an author earns you *instant credibility* from family, friends, colleagues, podcast listeners, and customers.

#4: Everyone has NOT figured it out yet.

Most podcasters and business owners are "too busy" to write and publish a book, mistakenly believe that it takes tens of thousands of sales to hit bestseller (more on this in a future Chapter), or they just do not fully realize the massive opportunity in front of them.

In fact, your competition is still spinning their wheels handing out boring business cards that get tossed, paying for banner ads that people ignore, and *wishing* for more publicity.

Now is the time to strike!

Pounce like a tiger (rawr!) on your chance to tell your story, share your experience, demonstrate your specialized expertise, promote your podcast, and stand head and shoulders above the crowd.

#5: The benefits are beyond what you think.

For myself and my clients, I have seen doors open and opportunities appear out of no where just because we had a book. You cannot plan for and anticipate them all. You have to just take forward action and believe.

CHAPTER SEVEN

MYTH 7: "No one will buy my book, so it's not worth the effort."

3 Benefits of "Connection"

BOOKS ARE CONNECTING

In January of 2018, I listened on audiobook to *Your One Word* by Evan Carmichael. [You can hear me tell more about it on Episode 107 of Copy That Pops here: copythatpops.com/107]

After thoughtfully going through the book's exercises, I realized that my 'one word' that has been a thread throughout my life through today and even into my podcast and business is: Connection.

I love connecting. I think that's what life is all about. I think that's what makes us all the most happy.

Therefore, let's look at 3 ways a book helps us to connect.

1. Connection to yourself and your inner genius

The act of writing a book proves to yourself that you actually know a lot about your niche.

Writing gives you immense clarity.

And becoming a published author raises your inner confidence.

You are awesome.

The effects of this alone are worth it all! A lack of confidence held me back from action in the past. Being a (bestselling) published author helped me immensely to raise my prices, step on stage, and more!

All these actions internal confidence opened me up to take? They lead to growing my podcast, increasing my brand awareness, raising my authority, and connecting me to more opportunities.

2. Connection to your current audience

There are a lot of people following you and listening quietly to your show, but they are not yet buying your products or services. A book is a lower barrier to entry into your funnel and ecosystem.

For as little as $0.99 (actually, you can give your book away for free too!) your audience can learn more about you and your expertise ...and turn into clients.

You can also use current clients, podcast listeners, and fans as case studies in your book. Shouting out clients, listeners, and fans will make them love you even more and share your work with others.

3. Connection to new traffic

Amazon, as we already saw, is massive and a fabulous search engine. It's a place for new traffic to discover you.

And because "cold traffic" may not be ready to buy your pricier products and services, your book is a perfect top-of-the-funnel marketing tool. It's a low investment from new traffic that can turn into new clients, listeners, and fans.

You are awesome.

Okay, But What If It Helps ONLY ONE Person?

You may still be stressed out thinking that you don't have a lot of people lined up and ready to buy your book (head over to CopyThatPops.com/training for a free 1-hour video training that will show you how you can still hit bestseller even without a huge email list. We'll also touch on this in Myth 8).

But, before diving into that, I want to analyze "what if your book helps ONLY ONE person" — is it still worth your time? Your effort?

JUST ONE IS STILL WORTH IT

You likely don't realize it yet. You probably can't fathom it.

But, your book is NEEDED for by someone else. [By many someone elses.]

Other people are *waiting* for your message, your personal stories, and your book to start their dreams.

Other people are searching for someone they connect with to be inspired to action. But, they aren't finding who they are searching for. Why? Because *you* haven't written your book yet.

I know that can sound a bit cheesy, but it's true.

It may not happen right away, but I promise you FOR A FACT that someone at some point will come up to you and thank you for your book because it impacted their life.

I swear it.

So, you can't quit for that one person (and the many, many others who may think it but never tell you).

Even if your book helps just one person, it's worth it.

You are awesome.

Okay, But What If Truly NO ONE Buys My Book?

The absolute worse case scenario running amok in your head is, "What if NO ONE buys the book?"

No one buys it, no one likes it, and no one thanks you for it. Maybe you even get some spiteful comments from trolls about the book on Amazon and Facebook. [Oh, no!] :)

Worse case scenario, right?

Although this worse case scenario is not going to happen, let's look more closely at it to pinpoint all the amazing booky benefits you'll still enjoy, even if you make $0 in book sales.

#1: You Win or You Learn

I don't believe that selling 0 copies is a 'loss.' I believe it's a 'learn.'

If TRULY zero people cared about your book's contents, that doesn't mean you shouldn't be a published author. It doesn't mean you suck.

It just means you should pick a different topic. Or do more for marketing to the right audience.

You aren't the problem, it's your topic or promotion. Lesson learned! Do it again or share it with different people.

#2: You Took Awesome Action

At least you took ACTION! So many folks talk a big game, do nothing, and then try to drag others down because they feel insecure.

Not you! You *did* something to move forward.

And action begets action. It begets results. Feel the energy and power that comes from not just daydreaming, but actually DOING.

I'm proud of you. :)

#3: Legacy

By publishing a book, you get something that your grandkids, your great-grandkids, and beyond can reference back to.

Oh, how I WISH that my great-great-grandma wrote something, ANYTHING, that I could read today. What a priceless gift that would be!

#4: You Are Still a "Published Author"

Even if you sell 0 copies of the book, you are still a published author on Amazon.

You are awesome.

This will make you sound cool a cocktail parties, networking events, and family get-togethers. *So worth it.*

It will also add credibility to your podcast, add flare to your bios, and make you more attractive as a public speaker...which brings us to...#5.

#5: Mo' Money, Mo' Money, Mo' Money

If you ACTUALLY sell 0 copies of the book, you can (and should, if you make *any* effort at all) still make thousands of dollars (or more, depending on your lifetime value of a client) with your book.

Gasp

How?

1. Free speaking gigs
- Where you grow your email list, expand your podcast listenership, and sell your products or services.
- You can also sell or give away your book for free and sign them! This makes you look like a rock star and helps build your audience and leads.

2. Paid speaking gigs (where you also may be able to sell from the stage)
- Some events have 'published a book' as a prerequisite to being allowed to speak on stage.
- A professional speaker told me that those who have published books are paid more than speakers without books.

3. Media opportunities that put you in front of more people, bigger audiences, and the 'right' connections to set up

things you cannot even fathom right now
- Leverage the fact that YOU wrote THE book on "XYZ topic" to get interviews on podcasts, local TV, local radio, local newspapers, online publications, industry magazines, guest blogs, Facebook Live shows, YouTube channels, virtual summits, joint venture webinars, and more for thousands of dollars worth of free media attention.
- All that extra attention will lead to more traffic, leads, and sales.
- And proof of local news features can be leveraged to get national outlets too.

4. Free + Shipping Funnel (a la Russell Brunson with Click Funnels)
- This is where the upsells you offer actually make you a profit over costs and advertising, if you do it right. I'll link out examples is the Reader Bonuses: CopyThatPops.com/BookBonuses

5. Give the book out free as a gift
- It's like a business card on steroids.
- No one will toss it in the trash bin when they get home and it's major credibility time and time again.
- If you don't land business from this, you are not giving your book to the right people.

6. Baller bios
- Update your LinkedIn bio, website About page, Media page, and email signature to reflect your new "Published Author" or "Amazon Bestselling Author" status

7. Raise your prices
- Earn more money per hour, per client, per sale with raised rates. The more credibility indicators you have, the more you're justified in charging premium prices.

You are awesome.

TO SUM IT ALL UP

The absolute worse case scenario is literally not going to happen.

But if it did... is it REALLY that bad?

Not at all!

I know you've grown through worse things.

And you stand to gain so much, even if you sell 0 copies! It's a no-lose scenario!

CHAPTER EIGHT
MYTH 8: "I could NEVER hit bestseller."

You are awesome.

What Is A Bestseller Anyhow?

THE IMPOSSIBLE DREAM?

When I first thought about becoming a #1 bestseller (back in 2016 with my first book *Copywriting for Podcasters*), it seemed like an impossible dream.

I didn't have a big email list.

I didn't have money for ads (or time to figure them out).

All I had was about 1,800 friends on Facebook.

Still something! But from that, there was NO WAY I'd be able to sell tens of thousands…or millions???..of copies to outrank all the amazing, top-notch bestsellers like Tim Ferriss, Gary Vee, and Oprah in nonfiction and famous novels from J.K. Rowling, Dickens, and Cervantes in fiction?

If you look at Wikipedia's dynamic list of the best selling books of all time, you start to get a sense of how difficult it is to actually track the most-sold books.
(Source: en.wikipedia.org/wiki/List_of_best-selling_books)

And think about it--if bestseller lists only counted "Most Books Sold, Ever," then every week the *New York Times* would publish a list that started with Don Quixote and ended with Alice in Wonderland.

Kind of a waste of space, and not super helpful for any new authors! ;)

But then bestseller lists on their own get...even fuzzier.

It might seem like they're put together in a vacuum that's perfectly objective. They give off an air of authority. Surely the #1 slot on the *New York Times* bestseller list was filled by the best possible book of the current cultural moment, right?

But wait, then what about the *Wall Street Journal's* bestseller list, *USA Today's* bestseller list, or *Publisher's Weekly's* bestseller list?

Why aren't all those #1 books the same, if they're all national lists pulling 'the must accurate data'?

The thing is, with all these lists, they're put together by people. And we all know that people are biased. Let's focus on the *New York Times* bestseller list as an example for how these lists tend to work.

HOW THE *NEW YORK TIMES* BESTSELLER LIST ACTUALLY WORKS

The *New York Times* bestseller list only counts sales from a secret, select group of bookstores. The metrics reported on their website are a little vague, as seen below:

"Rankings reflect unit sales reported on a confidential basis by vendors offering a wide range of general interest titles. Every

week, thousands of diverse selling locations report their actual sales on hundreds of thousands of individual titles. The panel of reporting retailers is comprehensive and reflects sales in stores of all sizes and demographics across the United States."
- *New York Times* Bestseller Methodology

(Source: nytimes.com/books/best-sellers/methodology)

It's unclear if the "thousands of diverse selling locations" are the same as "the panel of reporting retailers," but I have a hunch the actual panel is much smaller.

They update their rankings every week, and it's not uncommon for people to buy their way onto the list--or the other major lists, like *Washington Post* or *USA Today*.

(*Source: www.tim.blog/2012/08/17/amazon-monthly-100*)

Let's just say that if you:
• are able to get 5,000-10,000 pre-orders or purchases in your launch week
• have a deal with one of the big New York publishing houses, and
• know toward which book stores to skew those purchases

…you can hit the list, even if those purchase are gamed.

If you don't have the above, 99.5% chance you will not hit the list.

HOW IS AMAZON DIFFERENT?

1. Most importantly, Amazon's bestseller rankings aren't manually decided by people.

It's algorithmic.

2. Amazon bestseller rankings are category-specific — and, more accurately, *subcategory*-specific.

That means to be a #1 Amazon Bestseller, you don't have to outsell everyone in the "Biographies and Memoirs" category, or even everyone in the "Professionals and Academics" subcategory.

Your focus would be 3 tiers down--on the "Business" subsection of the "Professionals and Academics" subcategory of the "Biographies and Memoirs" parent category.

The narrower you get, the less competition you'll have. And, thus, the fewer sales you'll need to top that subcategory.

You are awesome.

[Screenshot of Amazon Best Sellers page showing "Crushing It in..." by Brian H Murray, Paperback, $23.98, ranked #1 in Books > Business & Money > Real Estate > Sales, Mortgages, and #1 in Books > Textbooks > Business & Finance > Real Estate. Amazon Best Sellers Rank: #3,461 in Books.]

So, this book is ranked #1 in 3 subcategories under Real Estate, under Business & Money, under Books.

3. The One Hour Rule

Not only does Amazon count its bestsellers in these narrow categories, but it also updates every *hour*. Why? Amazon wants to show its customers the most up-to-date and relevant information possible.

So maybe you think you couldn't outsell Sheryl Sandberg (the COO of Facebook)--and you're probably right.

But release your book on a slow day, when no other major releases are planned, in categories that are relevant but not crazy competitive, and chances are that for ONE HOUR, you could outsell the other books in your category.

This isn't "most sales over time," either — it's calculated with *recent sales.*

So if, during the last hour, 25 people bought your book, and 13 people bought a different book, you're coming out on top — even though the numbers you're playing with are small.

4. Paid and free books on Amazon are weighted the same — but they have separate bestseller lists.
(*Source:* makeuseof.com/tag/8-things-people-dont-know-amazons-bestsellers-rank-sales-rank)

So if you're selling your book for $2.99, you don't have to worry about someone giving away their book for free and taking over your slot.

WHY IS AMAZON LIKE THIS?

Well, Amazon sells thousands of products. And "bestseller" isn't a title limited to books — every other product category runs off the same metrics.

So whether you're looking for an indepth how-to book or a really good detergent, something in every category is going to be a "bestseller."

Amazon says this about their Bestseller List:

"*While the Amazon Bestsellers list is a good indicator of how well* a product is selling overall, it doesn't always indicate how well an item is selling among other similar items. Category and subcategory best seller lists were created to highlight an item's rank in the categories or subcategories where it really stands out."

(Source: amazon.com/gp/help/customer/display.html?nodeId=525376)

You are awesome.

33, Are You Kidding Me?

33 BOOK SALES

Yuppers.

So, you may be wondering how many sales I had when I hit #1 in "Podcasts & Webcasts" with my first book *Copywriting for Podcasters* in both the US and Canada at the end of 2016.

I did it with 33 sales. *gasp*

Permission to Write a Brand Building Book For Podcasters

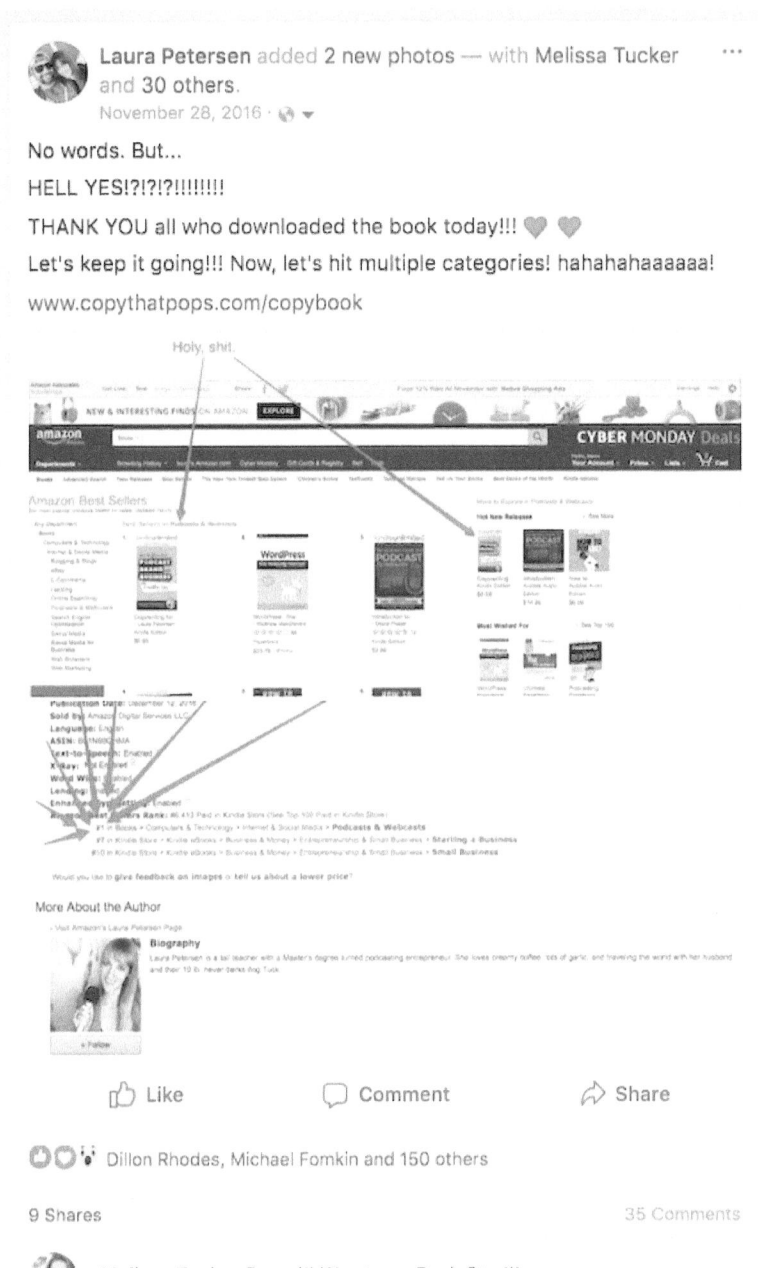

So, all this to say...

You are awesome.

#1: You absolutely can get to the top of a relevant subcategory for your own book.

#2: Even though it's easier than you likely ever imagined, it's still worth it. Not convinced? Go to Myth 9! :)

CHAPTER NINE

MYTH 9: "Well, Amazon bestseller is meaningless now, so why bother?"

You are awesome.

Don't Hate The Playah

IT'S ALL AN INSIDE GAME

First of all, the more you play the games of life, business, and the arts, the more you see 'inside' that things are rigged for those with money, power, and/or powerful connections.

That's not to be nihilistic or negative.

That's just to say that nothing is actually that big of a deal (so, calm down :-P) and nothing is as objective or difficult to achieve as you thought. To me, that means that your life isn't over if you don't achieve some external 'signal' of success *and* you are not a superstar if you do. For me, this alleviates some of the pressure.

Want to be a *New York Times* bestseller?

You can buy that.

So, how is hitting the *NYT* list any more 'valuable' that Amazon best seller? Sure, it takes more copies sold and money spent to do it. But I personally am not that impressed with either.

I care more if you are a good person and your book gives value to its intended audience.

HERE'S MY TAKE ON IT

You've gotta start somewhere. That "somewhere" might as well be #1 Bestseller in your subcategory, for as long as you can keep it.

If that's an hour? Fine! It's all about building gradual momentum.

And it still takes effort.

PLUS, A BOOK IS JUST A TOOL

Ultimately, I see a book as a great tool to:

1. Share value with a narrow audience (who I want to convert into listeners, fans, customers, or collaborators)

2. Prove authority in a subject matter (and books still contribute to that aim, no matter what lists they appear on)

3. Leverage for more opportunities that grow your podcast, personal brand, and business (read: money, status, media attention, etc.)

So, to achieve 1-3 above, I would argue that hitting #1 in a category on Amazon -- while not as hard as on *NYT* -- is still proof that you got out of bed, made an effort, and hit a goal.

So, just do it. Haters be damned.

How?

That's a subject for a future book!

You are awesome.

But I DO have resources already publicly available on my blog and podcast. CopyThatPops.com/blog and CopyThatPops.com/podcast.

And, of course, you can hire me to help you. #Shocker

Part Three

QUIETING THE 'SENIOR PRINCESSES' [I.E. HATERS INSIDE & OUTSIDE YOUR HEAD]

You are awesome.

CHAPTER TEN
How I Overcome Self-Doubt & Haters

You are awesome.

The Mean Girls

To meet me now, you may mistakenly think that I never felt insecure, self-doubt, or Imposter Syndrome. Not true.

Actually, I still feel it, but fighting each day not to let it slow me down.

But, if I think back to when I first realized something important about overcoming self-doubt and haters, we'd need to travel back to the decade of the best music ever…

LEMME TAKE YOU BACK TO 1999

Back in high school we had major cliques…and the prettiest, most popular girls ran the school.

Know what I'm talking about?

If you grew up in a small town or smaller school, maybe you didn't have this so much…but picture the movie *Mean Girls* with Lindsay Lohan. In that film, Rachel McAdams (who's a revelation!) was the leader of the mean girls in their school.

That's what I'm talking about.

I grew up in The OC -- like ohmygawd totally! -- and as you can probably imagine, all the "cool girls" had flashy new cars, wore designer clothes, and rocked fake nails and too much makeup.

The popular girls from the senior class were seen as gods. Envied and adored and obeyed.

Year after year, the god-like senior girls:
• lead the student council
• won all the spots in the Homecoming royalty
• dominated the photos in the yearbook
• and were spotlighted in every single school assembly

My graduating class...the Class of '99...started out no differently. The self-selected elite rose to power and prominence as in all the years prior.

They got all the attention and perks due their roles and stature. But, it got worse…

You are awesome.

Senior Princess Oppression

POPULAR, PINK, AND MEAN

There was one other tradition each year I haven't mentioned yet.

And this...this, is where things get interesting...

So, the popular girls always made t-shirts for themselves proclaiming their coolness and wore them with pride, delighting in excluding everyone else.

My year, they selected the name "Senior Princesses" atop hot pink shirts. "On Wednesdays we wear pink." The Mean Girls movie must have know about our Senior Princesses.

[I'll include a short clip from the movie in the Reader Bonuses, for your entertainment].

The Senior Princesses shoved their superiority in everyone's faces. It was all fun and games if you were a 'chosen one,' but if not, you were a second or third class citizen at my school.

BUT THEN...

But then, one day I arrived to hear a buzz whipping through the school! The face of every Senior Princess was hot pink with rage. (no pun intended ;))

Their eyes pierced like daggers at all who passed.

'What had happened?' I wondered.

[From this, you can see I was not a Senior Princess…far from it…I was in the AP / Honors nerd group…the group of kids who competed to get A's and joined clubs just to pad their college applications and go to an ivy league school. No cool shirts for us!] haha

But back to the story…

Enter: The Senior Queens

THE REIGN OF TERROR IS CHALLENGED

That one fateful day, the geekiest of geeky girls at our school (who in our case were the band kids and color guard gals) had printed shirts of their own.

The shirts were purple.

And they read:

"Senior Queens"

Oh, the uproar!

You could cut the tension in our school with a knife for days.

The Senior Princesses appealed to the student council, the principal, popular teachers, and the school staff. They demanded the Senior Queens be forbidden from wearing their shirts because it was THEIR tradition and only THEY could decide who was cool or not.

Only *they* could choose who got shirts.

Lessons Learned

MY BIG TAKEAWAYS

After the Senior Queens took their stand, more small groups of students started making their own shirts. It was amazing.

Eventually thought, it all blew over. The Senior Princesses were still mad, but there was nothing they could do so they just had to move on.

For me?

I never joined a clique that printed their own shirts.

As I watched it all unfold, I felt really proud of the Senior Queens for rejecting the idea that no one else was allowed to print shirts unless selected. It took courage to do what they did.

I realized that just because something was always done a certain way didn't make it right.

I vowed to never be:

1. A "Senior Princess" telling others they weren't good enough or allowed to do something

2. A person who put my own self in a box that 'isn't allowed' to do something and has to wait to be selected as 'worthy'

The Senior Queens taught me to STOP!
...waiting for permission...
...hoping to be chosen...
...wishing for more attention but doing nothing about it...
...allowing others to define me by exclusion...
...letting fear stand in my way...

The Senior Queens showed me:
You matter. You are worthy. You have something to share.

LET'S BRING IT BACK TO MODERN DAY

Nearly 20 years later, and I still see myself and others in boxes. That's why I wanted to write this book. I still see myself and others believing we aren't ready, expert enough, good enough, pretty enough, etc... to step into the light and move our lives, podcasts, brands, and businesses forward.

What I am working on now?

I'm focused on getting out of my self-imposed "scared of public speaking box." We all have areas of growth. :) Look out for a book on *Public Speaking That Pops!* in the near future!

I already tackled my, 'do I have permission to write a book?' obstacle.
[I'll tell you that story in the next section to inspire and motivate you further!]

Spoiler Alert:
I wrote my first book, self-published it, marketed it with no ad

budget, and hit #1 bestseller in my category on Amazon of "Podcasts and Webcasts."

I printed my "Published Author" shirt! BOOM!

[And you will too].

CHAPTER ELEVEN
My New Manifesto

"Print Your Own Shirt"!

HOW TO PRINT *YOUR* OWN SHIRT

To tie this story into your book writing ambitions, let's talk about a few "don'ts"!

• Don't wait for a publisher to select you and tell you you're allowed to write and publish a book.

• Don't wait for an arbitrary number of fans on Facebook or Instagram to deem you eligible to share your expertise and passion.

• Don't wait for an arbitrary number of podcast downloads to say you're 'expert enough now.'

• Don't listen to 'traditionally published authors' scoff and throw scorn at being proud of hitting bestseller in a subcategory in Amazon.

• Don't let the fears and insecurities of friends and family persuade you not to write a book.

In high school we feel bullied and trapped in cliques and groups. But as adults, we get to choose.

You are awesome.

As podcasters, entrepreneurs, content creators: We *must* be brave and question 'rules' and 'norms.'

Just because past rules applied to book writing and publishing, doesn't mean they do anymore.

There are a lot of "Senior Princesses" out there who will tell you that you can't speak on stage...you shouldn't write a book...you aren't good enough to do XYZ.

Often times that "Senior Princess" is in YOUR OWN HEAD.

Completely self-imposed.

What 'Senior Princesses' and made up 'traditions' are stopping you from printing *your own* shirt? Sharing your message? Spreading your light?

OKAY, HERE'S MY POINT FOR YOU: THE MANIFESTO

The bottom line is this...

...Everyone has value and a story to share.
...There is never a more perfect time to start than right now.
...A book doesn't have to be your life's work (as we discussed earlier, think of it more as a great collection of blog posts or repurposed podcast episodes on one topic in your zone of genius).
...You don't have to wait for a publisher to give you an offer, for someone else to tell you you're ready, or for your shoulder to be tapped. But if you feel like you need this, this book IS your permission. You now have it. Blame me if anything goes awry.

At the end of the day...

… Print your own damn shirt!

• Want to be an author? ...Print your own shirt!

• Want to hit bestseller on Amazon? ...Print your own shirt!

• Want to be seen as an expert in your niche? ...Print your own shirt!

You with me!?!?

What will be on your shirt?

• "I am a best selling author"
• "I am a non-fiction author"
• "I am a published author"
• "I am an authority in _____"

See those words in your mind and hit PRINT.

Your shirt is being made!...The machine spins and whirls with the final touches...you reach out to grab it in your hands and feel the soft cotton, slip it over your head, and BAM!

Wear your shirt with pride.

And then, when you're ready, I invite you to help others do the same. Pass this book on to someone else who needs it next.

You are awesome.

Part Four

My Story: Book #1 and Beyond

You are awesome.

CHAPTER TWELVE
Sick Of Feeling Like a Nobody = Massive Action

You are awesome.

Fall of 2016 Was A New Chapter

THE STORY OF MY FIRST BOOK

I taught high school Math and Psychology for about 5 years before taking the full leap into entrepreneurism.

That jump was in 2011.

Flash forward to 2016...

In April, after already working on and launching podcasts for clients, I started my own podcast Copy That Pops and was releasing about 6 episodes a month.

By the Fall, I'd then been working *hard* for 5 years as a business owner, 2 years as a podcast producer, and about 6 months as a podcaster.

But I felt stuck...

I felt burned out and invisible...

I felt frustrated and embarrassed that my business and podcast weren't growing as fast as I felt like they should be.

So, in October of that year, I decided that I had enough of

'playing small' and said I'd do whatever it took to never feel like this again! I wanted clients to come TO ME instead of feeling like I was always chasing.

I dove into conferences, meet-ups, and events to improve my network.

But what I found was that people would look around the room for 'bigger' names to jump over to while pretending to talk to me.

That hurt.

Business cards seemed to be a complete waste of time. If you were anyone 'of note,' people sought you out to take a selfie, invite you on their podcast, or hire you. If not, you were seen as 'a needy newbie' and generally overlooked or dismissed.

I started to notice that most all of the speakers and 'influencers' in these events had a book.

It made me realize that books were the new calling card. Business cards were tossed in the trash. But people treated a book with reverence. And the author was *instantly* seen as an expert. Someone important.

And those who could claim "bestseller"? Woah, even more so!

One evening at an event, I had the chance to ask a question of James Altucher, who I mentioned earlier as an influencer who has self-published.

Altucher has both had publishing deals with major publishers and gone it alone via Amazon. He's earned millions of dollars and started multiple super successful businesses. He also has a hugely popular podcast and hilarious blog.

He knows what he's talking about!

So, in his reply to me he said (paraphrasing):
"If you want to stand out and grow your brand and authority, you should write and self-publish a book."

He was the third person to advise me to write a book in one week! It was like the universe hit me over the head. Third time's a charm.

Right then and there I decided to take massive action and write a book.

30 days later on 11/28/16 I had written, self-published, and marketed (without an ad budget or email list) my first book called *Copywriting for Podcasters*, which hit #1 bestseller in BOTH the US and Canada in the category "Podcasts & Webcasts."

Was it worth the effort?

CHAPTER THIRTEEN
Amazing Rewards!

You are awesome.

Brand and Business Building Results From Bestselling Book

SOME GREAT RESULTS

Here are just *some* of the things that have happened to me since I took action, wrote a book, and hit #1 bestseller in a relevant category.

All of it builds brand!

All of it leads to more growth, sales, and impact.

IN PRINT
- Featured in Arianna Huffington's *Thrive Global*
- Authored articles in both *Thought Leader* and *Accelerant* magazines

USING AUDIO
- Invited onto tons of podcast shows (too many to count — see CopyThatPops.com/media for an up-to-date list)
- Interviewed John Lee Dumas of *EOFire* (twice) for my podcast on Episode 052 and 056 [CopyThatPops.com/052 & CopyThatPops.com/056]

You are awesome.

WITH VIDEO
• Attended TV & film premieres and walked red carpets with idols of mine
• Helped on set in St. Petersburg, Florida with Greg Rollett, an Emmy-Award winning Producer, during filming of the Emmy-Award nominated show *Ambitious Adventures* with Caleb Maddix, Matt Maddix, and Kevin Harrington (of *Shark Tank*)
• Helped on set in Hollywood filming an interview with Brandon T. Adams (co-star in the film *Think & Grow Rich: The Legacy*) and Brian D. Evans (Founder of *Influencive*)

ON STAGE
• Spoke on stage on podcasting, copywriting, and publishing bestselling books on Amazon
• Spoke on stage on the Podcast Cruise (by founders of Podcast Movement!), Ultimate Stage Experience, Massive Success Breakthrough, and more in the works!
• Led Pat Flynn's mastermind group in San Diego during his absence (twice)
• Taught a lesson for Podcast Movement's virtual all access pass
• Invited to be an expert speaker to the Podcast Success Summit

- Helped run behind the scenes of the Live Stage at Social Media Marketing World 2018

The snowball effect of this makes me feel proud, extremely confident, and more in control of my own business now being seen as a leader and not a follower.

It all started with the book.

But who else has done it too? Go next to Part 5 with Case Studies!

You are awesome.

PART FIVE

YOU ARE NOT ALONE - 7 CASE STUDIES OF PEOPLE LIKE YOU

You are awesome.

Case Study 1: Sabah Ali (20 Year-Old College Student & Podcaster)

You are awesome.

Permission to Write a Brand Building Book For Podcasters

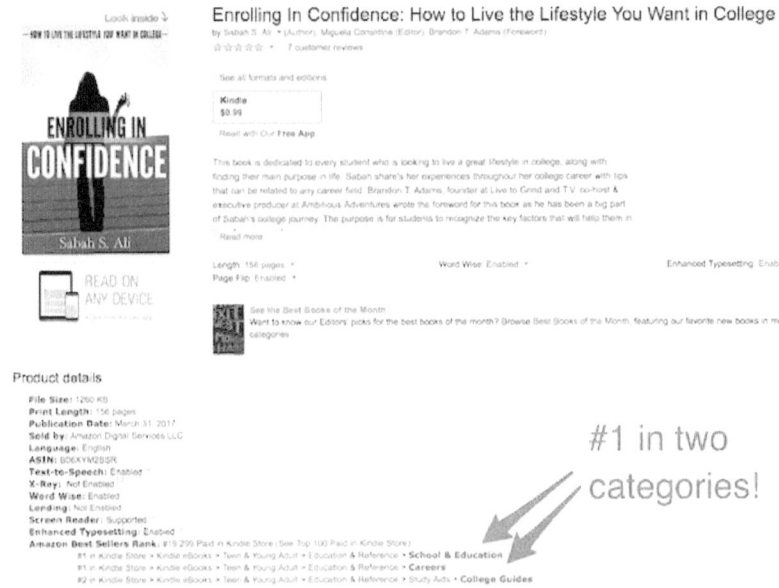

Sabah Ali was *still in college* (in a small town in Iowa) when she was the co-host of a podcast and, while working with me, hit #1 Bestseller on Amazon in two categories plus #1 Hot New Release in all three of her categories with her book *Enrolling in Confidence*.

It was her first book and she did it all in 30 days: writing, self-publishing, and hitting bestseller.

You can check out her book here: CopyThatPops.com/Sabah

RESULTS FROM THE BOOK:

• Sabah was featured on the COVER of the *Iowa State Daily* newspaper
• Sabah went on live TV (twice so far)
• Sabah booked her first paid speaking gig
• Sabah decided to launch her Instagram Digital Agency and has

You are awesome.

already booked clients impressed by her book and media features

And this is JUST the beginning for her!

Now, she is growing an Instagram Digital Agency. Think she can charge more as a 'bestselling published author' than without that bragging right?

You betcha.

Permission to Write a Brand Building Book For Podcasters

You are awesome.

Sabah Ali: blogger, student, entrepreneur, etc.

by CBS2/Fox 28 Staff | Thursday, February 15th 2018

YOUR TAKEAWAY:

Just because you are 'young' or 'new' or 'not as far as big names in your field' doesn't mean you don't have value to share.

It doesn't mean you don't have expertise in *your* experiences and realms.

In fact, you are a better teacher to those 2 steps behind you than 'experts' who are 20 steps ahead of you (because that's 22 steps ahead of the reader and they forgot what it feels like to 'not know' — they're too out of touch to help the reader like you can)!

So, why are you holding yourself back if even college students are taking action and using their books to land speaking gigs around the country, get on live TV, and blow up their brands!?

It's your turn!

Case Study 2: Tom Camp (Musician, Podcaster, & Digital Nomad)

Permission to Write a Brand Building Book For Podcasters

You are awesome.

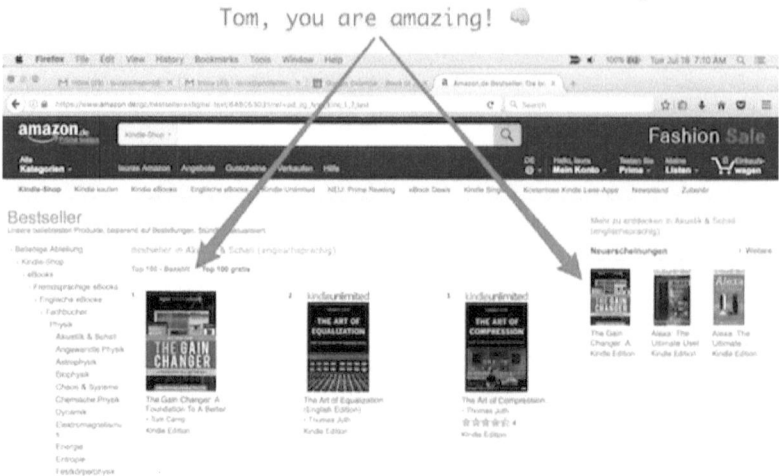

Tom, originally from New Jersey, was living abroad with his girlfriend and their three cats in Thailand.

As a digital nomad and podcaster, he focuses on helping musicians get radio-ready mixes.

After he saw me write my first book, he decided to jump into my course and publish his first book. *The Gain Changer* was born! And it hit #1 Bestseller on Amazon in all three categories in the United States, plus #1 in a category in Germany too.

You can check out his book here: CopyThatPops.com/Tom

RESULTS FROM THE BOOK:

- Industry influencers are reaching out to Tom!
- Tom grew his email list
- Tom developed a connection with his new tribe and people started emailing him thanking him for his valuable advice
- Tom booked more clients from the exposure of his book launch.

He says, "I went from skilled guy taking no action to closing big deals practically overnight"
• And, with ZERO ongoing marketing effort, his book is selling 2-5 copies per day

And this is JUST the beginning for Tom!

YOUR TAKEAWAY:

It doesn't matter where you are living. And it doesn't matter if you have a big email list already or not (Tom, Sabah, and I all didn't!).

What matters is that you care about sharing helpful information with people who are a couple steps behind you and would be your ideal clients, partners, or fans.

Take action forward and opportunities will come along (like they did for Tom) that you can't even predict, but will surely be thankful for.

It's your turn!

Case Study 3: Mitch Durfee (Growing Public Speaker)

Permission to Write a Brand Building Book For Podcasters

You are awesome.

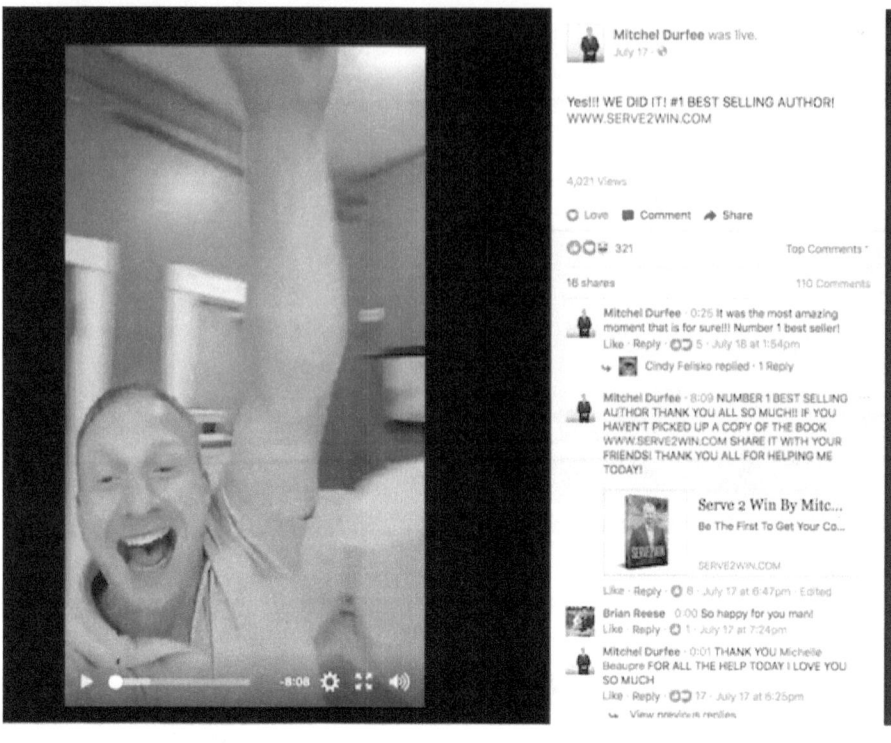

Mitch Durfee is a veteran turned serial entrepreneur who is passionate about serving others.

His book was mostly completely when we started working together on the copy for his cover and a marketing plan for his launch.

As a first time author, Mitch hit #1 Bestseller on Amazon in a Business category with his book *Serve 2 Win*!

You can check out his book here: CopyThatPops.com/Mitch

RESULTS FROM THE BOOK:

• Mitch told me, "The best selling book is what I call a great disrupter. Out of all the things I've accomplished the best seller holds the most weight hands down any day of the week."

• Mitch realized that speakers with books are more coveted and higher paid. That's part of what motivated him to take action to write and publish. Next, he's leveraging his book for more and more paid speaking gigs.

And this is JUST the beginning for Mitch!

YOUR TAKEAWAY:

Writing a book may not be a childhood dream of yours. But it can really catapult your speaking career and more. Like Mitch said, a book holds the most weight as compared to other things you can do to raise your status.

Another friend of mine in the National Speaker Association, who earns 5-figure speaker's fees per talk, told me that speakers who are authors get booked more and are paid more.

I've even heard of some stages that have a book as a prerequisite to be eligible for speaking.

So, if you want more stage time, get that book published!

It's your turn!

Case Study 4: David France (Superconnector & Philanthropist)

Permission to Write a Brand Building Book For Podcasters

You are awesome.

David France is a professional violinist, the Founder of the Roxbury Youth Orchestra, and a super connector. He wrote *Show Up!*

As a first-time author and, after taking my Masterclass course, he hit #1 Bestseller on Amazon in both the US and in Canada.

The book is STILL #1 as I write this 4 months after his publication.

You can check out his book here: CopyThatPops.com/David

RESULTS FROM THE BOOK:

I asked David to share with me a bit about the results he's seen from becoming an author. Here is what he shared with me (on March 21, 2018…just 4 months after publishing his book)…

1. "A few weeks ago I walked into Google's Boston office and of the recent candidate for Mayor was the keynote speaker. After the talk, I went up to say hello and he turned to the group he was with and said, 'Only ONE person in this circle is a Best-Selling

Author!' I was honored and SOO surprised he knew!!!"

2. "People start marketing YOU and your book because they are proud of you and honored to know you"

3. "Speaking Engagements: I was offered a keynote *while* writing the book and was offered 2 more within 2 months of writing the book."

4. "Podcasts: I have now been a guest on 6 shows including one internationally in Ireland and have been asked to be on 5 more shows in the next few months!"

5. "Coming to mind: You start coming to mind for other opportunities. For example, I got an email today about being nominated by a prestigious Boston university for a BIG award. I'm being flown across the country by someone who was following my book progress to perform a world-premier piece. And I've been asked to perform a Concerto with an orchestra next year."

6. "Fan mail: I've received emails from around the country and the world from people who enjoyed the book and wanted more resources or asked about getting coaching from me!"

7. "People have found me on LinkedIn and sent me a message after reading the book."

8. "When I meet people and tell them I've written a book they immediately jot it down in their notes and some have gone on Amazon and purchased it while i'm standing there!"

9. "Friends start asking for advice on book publishing and referring you to people in their network who are writing a book."

You are awesome.

And this is JUST the beginning for David!

YOUR TAKEAWAY:

Holy cow, David is doing amazing things with his book and author status! And so much of it is coming *to him* without much effort!

But the majority of these opportunities are completely unexpected. David couldn't have planned for them or known in advance that they would come.

He just took decisive action forward (without waiting for external permission) and is reaping the massive rewards. All the while, he is truly helping and inspiring people around the world.

Now, it's your turn to do the same!

Case Study 5: Kolton Krottinger (Disabled Veteran)

You are awesome.

Kolton Krottinger has gone from living on couches, to beating anxiety, to building a successful business as a disabled veteran, and after taking my Masterclass, he hit #1 Bestseller on Amazon in all three of his categories in the US!

You can check out his book here: CopyThatPops.com/Kolton

RESULTS FROM THE BOOK:

I asked Kolton for a list of some things that have happened to him since releasing his book (in November of 2017) and here is what he said (in March of 2018):

- "I had tons of people approach me at Funnel Hacking Live telling me the book changed their life."

- "I had a doctor order 10 copies and put them in her lobby."

- "I built a free + shipping offer that attracted people around the world."

- "One person told me the book saved their life."

- "People love the fact that I'm not a doctor and I shared (as an average person) what worked for me. And they feel comfortable talking about anxiety now since I opened the door and paved the way."

- "I had the CEO of a tech firm that is a partner with Microsoft tell me he was able to better communicate his anxiety to his friends and family. They started treating him better and his anxiety is significantly better."

- "I was almost a mini celebrity for the book in Orlando, Florida and I've never even been there!"

- "I was able to open my radio show *Anxiety Hacker Radio* on KVGI with over 200,000 monthly active listeners."

- "Facebook gave me the verified public figure 'blue check' next to my name as an author / entrepreneur."

- "I feel legit and appreciated now since doing your Masterclass course. People almost see me as an influencer or person they can trust and relate to me."

And this is JUST the beginning for Kolton!

YOUR TAKEAWAY:

Kolton's book was not a business how-to book, but it still had a massive impact on the business community, on his friends and colleagues, and on his own brand.

Just like Kolton, if you share authentically about your personal journey (the up's and the down's!) you *will* impact others in ways you cannot fully imagine yet.

Don't hold back. Don't let fear (or anxiety) stop you. We are waiting for your stories, your lessons, your knowledge, and your passion.

It's your turn!

Case Study 6: Jaya M.K. (Podcaster & Expert In An Obscure Field)

Permission to Write a Brand Building Book For Podcasters

You are awesome.

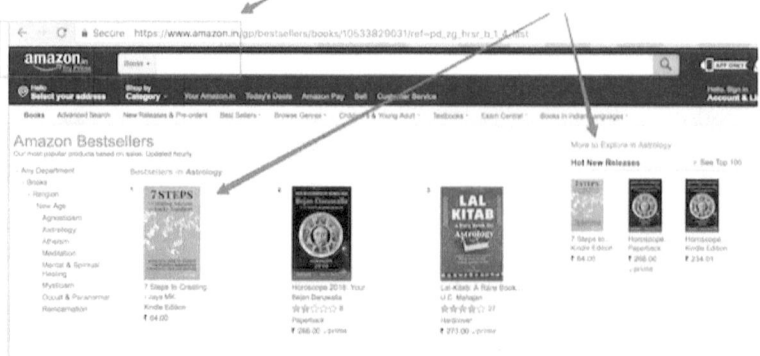

Jaya MK is a podcaster, life coach, and spiritual mentor. Her top passion is a field that is more obscure in the US but very popular in India and other countries in Asia: Numerology.

After taking my Masterclass course, Jaya launched her first book *7 Steps to Creating Success with Lucky Numbers* and hit #1 Bestseller on Amazon in India, Australia, the UK, and the US.

You can check out her book here: CopyThatPops.com/Jaya

RESULTS FROM THE BOOK:

• Jaya's authority as a numerologist skyrocketed. She was especially excited about hitting #1 in India, where numerology is very popular and practiced.
• Jaya told me that her book helped her create her brand.
• Jaya's book got her more engagement from her audience on podcast and social media
• Jaya reports a happy upward growth trend overall!

And this is JUST the beginning for Jaya!

YOUR TAKEAWAY:

No matter how 'niche' your topic is, a book is an incredible way to stand out, build your brand, engage your audience, and grow everything.

As Jaya discovered, a book is like fertilizer for everything else in your ecosystem. It helps grow your podcast, your social media engagement, your traffic, your sales, and your fans.

It's your turn!

Case Study 7: Akbar Sheikh (Very Busy Entrepreneur)

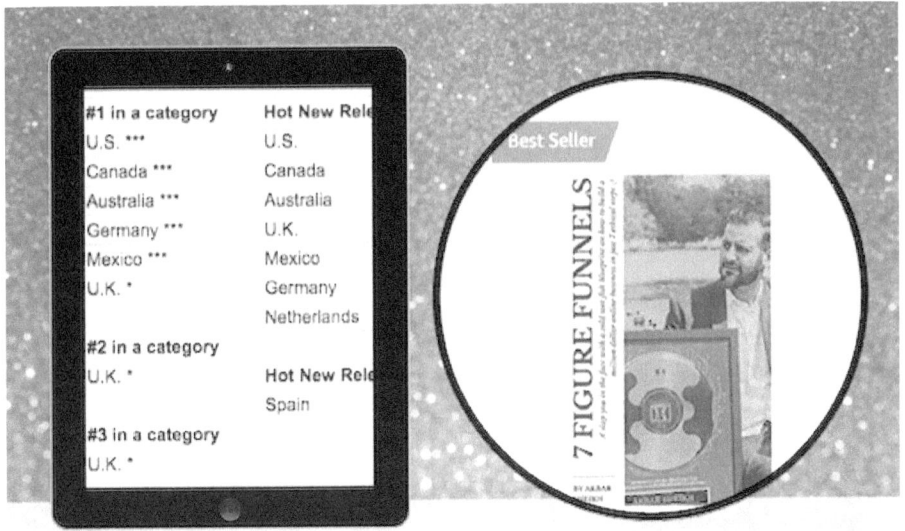

You are awesome.

Akbar is a very busy (and successful) entrepreneur with an incredible story of "homeless to 7 figure funnel building." But he had never written a book when we started working together.

With my help keeping the details on target and his ability to share in a connected way with his Facebook friends, Akbar was able to:

• Hit #1 Bestseller on Amazon in all three of his categories in FIVE COUNTRIES (US, Canada, Australia, Germany, and Mexico)
• Hit #1, #2, and #3 in his categories in a SIXTH country (UK)
• Find himself on the Hot New Release lists in EIGHT countries (US, Canada, Australia, Germany, Mexico, the UK, the Netherlands, and Spain)

You can check out his book here: CopyThatPops.com/AkbarBook

RESULTS FROM THE BOOK:

Direct quote from Akbar:
"*Being an author is instant authority. Instant credibility. It's a serious accomplishment. It just puts you on a whole different level.*"

What else has Akbar leveraged his book for?
- Akbar felt confident to raise his prices higher
- Akbar has landed even 'bigger fish' clients
- Akbar is getting asked to speak on more stages
- Akbar is getting more podcast interviews coming to him

And this is JUST the beginning for Akbar and his best selling book!

You are awesome.

YOUR TAKEAWAY:

Being busy is not an excuse to put off taking action on the incredible opportunity to become a bestselling author faster and easier than ever before.

Get help, outsource tasks you aren't great with (like editing, formatting, and graphic design), hire a coach, join an accountability group, and get 'er dunn! :)

It's your turn!

See More On The Wall Of Fame!

WALL OF FAME

Go to CopyThatPops.com/wall-of-fame for more case studies and a running feature of success stories like you!

I'd be honored to add you there someday soon.

If this book helps, please email me and tell me about it so I can feature you! Laura@CopyThatPops.com

Part Six

YOUR TURN, YOU AUTHOR, YOU!

You are awesome.

Your Permission Slip

Fill This Out!

I proudly accept

PERMISSION TO WRITE

a bestselling book

_____
(sign name here)

I'm ready to write, publish, & promote my book.

Today's Date:
_____

My Book Launch Date:
_____

Next Steps

TO REVIEW

In this book we have taken 2 quizzes, broken 9 myths, and looked at 7 case studies (plus my own story).

By now, it is my goal that you agree with me that:
1. You are ready, worthy, and 'enough' to write a book
2. Self-publishing is the way to go
3. There are so many ways to make your book work for you beyond book sales
4. Now is the time to take action

If you agree with all these, I have done my job. :)

BUT WHAT'S NEXT?

I have more books in the works that are 'how-to' in nature to help you take big steps forward from here.

But, in the meantime (or anytime!), if you are ready for MORE, I've got your back.

START HERE:

1. Reader Bonuses: <u>CopyThatPops.com/BookBonuses</u>
- Access to all link outs of this book in one place
- A real photo of the "Senior Princesses" you met in Part 3
- A real photo of me from high school
- Free 1-Hour Training Video on *How to Painlessly Write and*

You are awesome.

Publish A Best Selling Book on Amazon... With No Experience...In Under 8 Weeks...With $0 in Ads
• Free Facebook Group of like-minded new and aspiring authors who support each other before, during, and after book launch
• Free, helpful podcast episodes about books
• Epic blog posts to help you with all stages of your book journey
• 7 A's of Self-Publishing Checklist
• 5 Things You Must Do to Hit #1 Bestseller on Amazon
• And more!

2. BookThatPops.com will take you to a page on my website with more resources as well as ways to work with me more in-depth.

3. Talk with me on social media. I'm @LaptopLaura on Facebook, Twitter, and Instagram!
• Facebook.com/LaptopLaura
• Twitter.com/LaptopLaura
• Instagram.com/LaptopLaura

No matter what you do with your book writing journey, I hope that this book has given you the confidence and power to blaze forward.

I cannot wait to hear about your coming success.

Laura :)

PERMISSION TO WRITE A BRAND BUILDING BOOK

For Podcasters:
9 Myths Holding You Back
From More Exposure
& Making A Greater Impact

LAURA PETERSEN

The End.

Wait, why are you still reading?!
🤔

You are already awesome.
You are already good enough.
You are already an 'expert' to others.

Go and take action.

Stop overlearning, and start doing. :)~

Do This!

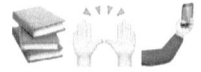

Tag me RIGHT NOW in a tweet, Facebook post, or Instagram story @LaptopLaura with what YOUR first book will be about! [I want to encourange you and hold you accountable!]

Then, get after it.
:)

www.ingramcontent.com/pod-product-compliance
Lightning Source LLC
Chambersburg PA
CBHW020655220526
45464CB00001B/448